Barb and Glen,

To Arci
experiences
part as ...
played a p..... ... Thank you'll remember
the evening that gave life to Appendix A.
Blessings always
Christmas, 2014
Much love,
Dan

of
1

A
SUDDEN
LONGING

The Making of a Charismatic

DAN R. BETTLE

Published by L'Horizon Press

ISBN: 978-1503337909

Graphic Design by Raina Pratt
rainapratt@gmail.com

TO SHERYL

For your love, as welcome as springtime

For your loyalty, as warm as light

For your laughter, the wine in our years

TABLE OF CONTENTS

METANOIA

I saw some burn with purity
   Beyond the meanness of the world,
Healing hearts, commanding bodies
   To conform to what they've heard.

As sparks to heaven fly,
   And the fire's gift warms all around;
So the burning ones do never care
   By whom the mystery is found.

Spirit, do not be a silent teacher;
   Train my speech to find the rhyme
In the singing of your purpose,
   As heard before, now in our time.

Then stay here, radiant Spirit,
   Warm my life, while still your flame
Follows harvest, cleanses stubble,
   And earth and heaven are the same.

– July, 2012

Metanoia: [Greek] - Repentance

ACKNOWLEDGEMENTS

There may have once been a writer who began his first work from a solitary impulse. But I can not believe any writer ends with something to offer the world without having received from many others a great deal of encouragement and useful criticism.

To my team there is only gratitude and thanks for the challenges and correctives you gave so willingly during the many months when I pushed and prayed toward a readable conclusion.   I hope I remembered to tell you personally as often as your contributions shaped my hours at the keyboard.

Cheers to all of you.

To Lorella Losa, Director of the Bellingham Healing Rooms, who was the first to read much of what is here and who insisted that I keep writing. You were teacher, mentor, and friend to a stranger who wanted only to inch closer to the fire.

To Herbert Douglass, President Emeritus of Atlantic

Union College, whose impulse to honor and faithfully encourage someone with whom he often disagrees makes him a paragon of courtesy and grace.

To my daughter, Catherine Madera, whose success as a writer gave her a strength to correct me that substantially improved the result. You shared many helpful insights while editing the text, books on the craft of writing, and resources needed for publishing. Without your prodding, my journal notes would have yellowed in my file cabinet unread.

To Jonathan Hanson, my pastor at Abundant Life, who understood immediately when I was overcome during worship time that it was my gift of worship to write what was streaming in my spirit.

To Darren Wilson, my special thanks for your generous permission to quote from *Filming God*.

And last because she is first in my affections, to my wife, Sheryl, whose voracious appetite for reading kept her company while I hammered away at 'the book' and who, in chorus with my daughter, never wavered in her conviction that I should share more of myself and preach less. No one could ask for a more supportive companion or more generous critic.

A WORD TO THE READER

Because of the unusual nature of Spirit-life, it's important to declare what this work is and what it is not.

This is not a memoir. It is a testimony. It covers only a five-year period, from January, 2008 to just beyond January, 2013. In flashbacks to certain events before 2008 I have shared experiences I believe prepared me to receive an unexpected gift of Presence. Then, one day God arrested me and I pray never again to be free. These are notes of a captive.

Regarding the format. I have made the individual sections thematic. Though for readability the incidents are arranged chronologically, they work more as illustrations than as a sequence. It has been a marker in these interruptions of the Kingdom of God that chronology is irrelevant; eternity flows as an ever present Now. I believe life in the Spirit is not measured by time as we know it – past, present, future – but by the level of intimacy we gain with the spiritual beings who relate to us.

To anchor the narrative I have used the place names where encounters with Spirit occurred. This has a Biblical precedent. Here is but one example. As Jacob limped away to face his brother after his historic all-nighter he called the place where he had wrestled with an angel till dawn, "Peniel." It means, "I have seen God face to face." We remember more easily the geographic place name – the Brook Jabbok.

When I was 14, I spent part of my Maine summer raking sea moss from submerged granite ledges a few feet off the high tide line of islands in Casco Bay. It was not for fun. There was a buyer for the wet moss at Lookout Point waiting for me and the few others in this odd seasonal trade. He told me the powdered moss was used as an emulsifier in the making of toothpaste and hand cream.

I loaded the moss into a 12' skiff, filling it until the gunwales were nearly awash, then slowly towed it to the buyer at the wharf. It was a delicate operation; one wrong move and a rolling skiff would take on water while I watched a day's work float away.

This book existed first as scraps of paper scribbled in haste while impressions were vivid. Notes made half asleep in a notebook by my bed, notes written in the margins of a church bulletin. Seeing the jumble I remembered my 12' skiff plowing along slowly at the end of a tow line, showing only 2" of freeboard. "I need to get this to the dock and offloaded before I lose it," I felt then. Spirit says to offload again. Thus, the book you hold in your hand.

INTRODUCTION

[His mercies] are new every morning;
great is your faithfulness.
Lamentations 3.22

The incidents you are about to read were a dramatic departure from the life I expected to live. Here is a long way from there. And the distance widens.

I could easily be convinced everyone's story is as strange to recall as mine. Perhaps everyone backs into their destiny as I have, bruised and mended. Perhaps it's normal for all lives to begin out of step and only much later fall into a steady rhythm.

In my case the stumbling stretched over six decades and three continents. It seemed I hopped a lot, always stepping out with confidence on my left foot but never sensing the following footfall of my right foot, to achieve an easy stride powered by a dominant strength.

Approaching the end of my seventh decade my right foot has fallen. My eighteen years of formal schooling are now infused by Spirit, balancing, finally, a long process of scholarship.

My Father has compelled me to know Him directly. Mingled with the joy of finding His version of myself, He has displayed a very wide and often shocking range of attributes. He has shown Himself humorous, playful, coy, jealous, surprising, curious and persistent. He is never cruel or indifferent but often imponderable in His compassion; at times loud and boisterous, then quiet and hidden. With my seminary education behind me I thought I would be doing post-graduate work only to realize I was enrolled in a new primary school.

My original purpose for writing was to simply download my class notes, so to speak. I never intended to write a confessional colored by emotions or to provide the backdrop of my personal story. I was concerned it might have the unintended consequence of drawing an unflattering contrast between my former life and the experiences that have followed. "All glory to God and leave me out of it" was to have been the theme. But redemption is a story only comprehended in all the circumstances of a full life yielded to that Author who writes grace large upon our pages.

Beyond the private sketches, I want even more to tell you about my invisible friend and why it's such a challenge to share what follows. An easy description is not possible. The Lord left us a disembodied Spirit for instructor, comforter, and power source, an I-can't-describe-it-but-it's-good gift. I was driven to ask the questions about the Lord's surrogate the disciples must have asked. Unfortunately, overcome by circumstances, they never left us their conclusions. Who is this Holy Spirit, this divine person who has no name? And what does this Holy Spirit want with me? As beguiling as the wind which is known by a hundred names but which has never been weighed or measured, where do I start describing a personal force who provokes such unexpected events?

"Now faith is the assurance of things hoped for, the conviction of things not seen." It is supremely difficult to describe the essence of faith, for it is the door to experience more personal than your own history, the first instrument that captures music more beautiful than the sound of your own name. The evidence received of a higher order of life is more real than the air in your lungs

17

or the blood in your veins. Why, then, does this downlink from a superior realm often vanish in an instant as soon as recognized? Is heaven so utterly 'Other' that our moments touched by glory must necessarily be brief? I ache to know. Not yet fully mature, I long for a greater measure of control. And I know I'm not alone, caught surprised in a no-man's-land between a rational adult and a child's sensations.

Indeed, the first help I received was from the bank of childhood memories. I realized now with the contrast of adult experience how little had been needed to sense the life in the natural world around me, how subtleties could so quickly lead me below the surface – the bent grass or snapped twig that showed where an animal had passed, the sharper cries of gulls when they've discovered food, the thin rime ice on leaves that proved the temperature overnight had fallen below freezing.

One of my initial insights was that subtlety is the franking mark of heaven. How do I know a letter sent to me went through the Post Office? Because the postage stamp has been canceled, we say; there is a franking impression across its face that gives the name of the Post Office where it was left for later delivery to me.

When heaven 'talks' to me, when my receiver picks up vibration at that level of reality higher up and further in, it is normally stamped or franked with an alternate and subdued energy. Its subtlety (familiar to anyone who's ever fallen in love), perversely, demands attention. Yet, the encounter is as easily lost as gained. I know myself free to reject it or receive it. The voice is never accompanied by a sense of duty or guilt or compulsion. Never! I am honored in the moment by such total freedom it has often been stunning. To know myself truly free is to sometimes sense a weight of judgment more profound than punishment.

But I will start with the obvious. Anyone this persistent wishes urgently to be known. I was touched, pushed, spoken to. I clearly sensed effect before I understood cause. I was thrown back to the primitive test I have instinctively used to determine if I should recognize another person – "I met someone, they moved me, and I ended up somewhere else."

Where I have ended up is with a friend who is unsuitable for polite company. My parents and mentors expected me to be punctual, reliable, and loyal. Holy Spirit (s/he has a name; you'll find the one I've chosen later) presents to me as a friend who is unpredictable, uncontrollable, and disrupts every agenda when present. The result is always good, provided I allow the 'good' to be defined by standards and circumstances I may only know much later, if at all. Yet, the relational flow is ultimately unequivocal, as irresistible in its unfolding beauty and power as a first love. Funny, but in the book of Revelation (2:4) we are reminded that an overwhelming "first love" is a spiritual standard.

However, as I saw in the stories of great saints, the relationship with Holy Spirit can be so intimidating that even the strong and the righteous are undone. It can also be a relationship of such idiosyncrasy that the human participant is incredulous. I am grateful for an introduction to Holy Spirit I could bear and am persuaded that in all our encounters with God's kingdom the boundaries of personhood are never breached, though they are constantly being moved.

I found two typical responses in encounters with Divinity; fear, often to the point of momentary terror, and back-talk. Fear is understandable. Being poked with a stick in the hand of a giant is threatening. But, strange as it seems on reflection, arguing with God is common.

Here's my short Bible list. Adam blames God for providing an imperfect wife. Moses tries every excuse to duck his commission as savior of his people and head of the clan. Later, at a crisis point, he confronts an immovable God until God changes His mind. Sarah laughs at an angel after being told a ninety year-old woman could bear children. Her husband bargains strenuously with angels until he's confident his nephew will be able to escape the destruction of Sodom. Job complains so loudly and so bitterly it takes four chapters to shut him up. Zechariah responds with a reflexive "Yeah, right!" to the angel bringing good news that his wife is going to become pregnant. One of the closest friends of Jesus, Martha, essentially reproaches Him for being late and missing the chance to save her brother. Humans must look like cartoons to angels whose sole purpose and delight is to do the Father's will.

I don't remember ever being enthusiastic about adventures with God. It was challenge enough to remain orthodox. As an undergraduate, my then fiancée and I were profoundly impacted by some after-hours Bible study with a former student. The doctrine we reviewed was the vibrant heart of the original gospels but the fervor of our friend's presentation was deemed by others to border on heresy. A private communication by a concerned faculty member to my family in Maine so disturbed my father he made an emergency trip to Massachusetts to meet with me. In the privacy of my dormitory room I saw deep emotion in my father for the first time. As he exhorted me to remain loyal to our faith community it brought tears to his eyes and a quaver to his voice.

At seminary my two favorite professors were made unwelcome and, under pressure for their audacity examining doctrinal assumptions, quietly slipped away to obscurity, leaving in their trail a whiff of brimstone. Several times before I earned my stripes at ordination I watched enthralled the drama of what happens when organizational foundations and dogma are artfully or pointedly examined.

The most momentous confrontation with authority involved a brilliant scholar of the New Testament who was on the faculty of one of the seminary's many feeder schools. He had condensed decades of study and class lectures into a compelling treatise remarkable both for its depth and its courage. The church leadership convened a conference at a remote summer camp for the sole purpose of giving his views a thorough airing. I was not invited, but for us cub preachers hanging on the outcome our waiting was as solemn as the crowds in St. Peter's square, hushed, watching the chimney smoke that shows the college of cardinals have given them a new pope.

The professor's exegesis was formidable, but his energy was a threat and his conviction a rebuke. In the few short days of the conference a coalition hardened in opposition and he was shown the door. He continued to preach and teach independent of the church's blessing and in a few years faded from view. But we seminarians just entering our careers came to understand that a long-term salaried future required no more of us than a shallow reading of scripture following clearly posted signage. In an organization whose DNA was to resist all fundamental change it was clear that the space for creativity was severely limited.

The sadder case that touched me personally was the downfall of a young and very popular religion professor in the South. He was only a few years my senior. He had what I could never hope to attain, a charisma projected by a warm baritone voice alive with the rich accent and rhythms of a South-Afrikaner. Hearing him preach was like dancing a slow waltz with a more agile and confident partner. He was one of us, an example of what the church said it wanted in the next generation. His teaching made St. Paul come alive and his delivery was electric. But his vocabulary was judged edgy and he was sent off to the wilderness of independent ministry where he established himself as an itinerant speaker.

There were others, too, whose adventures in theology made any wiggle room a dim prospect. One other provocateur in particular was seen off, quite literally, while I was in seminary. I laugh now, but the story is the closest thing to open transgressive behavior I could ever manage.

It was a bitter winter evening in southwestern Michigan. The night was given over to the annual faculty/board banquet, the most prestigious dress-up affair on our conservative campus. A former student, picking the venue and timing deliberately, had invited a controversial Australian layman to speak to any and all in the basement of the men's dormitory.

I lived in married student housing on the opposite corner of the campus. The news reached me shortly after he was introduced. I hurried over and had to stand

24

rows away from the speaker now completely surrounded by students enjoying every precious moment off the reservation. It was like watching one half of a boxing match, the speaker throwing precise verbal punches at absent opponents, some of whom were being feted only a few yards away.

It didn't last. A theology professor everyone respected had been tipped off and he arrived with a sullen campus security officer in tow. Not a single voice challenged the professor; he was the designated hit man for the concentration of hierarchy congratulating themselves in the lavishly decorated cafeteria a stone's throw away. The surreal moment passed and our guest was escorted off the grounds without protest. Mild stuff, I know, but I've never forgotten the adrenaline rush wondering if the rent-a-cop was going to take names.

However, my restraint was anchored in prejudices much deeper than merely my responses to the behavior of others. I was, after all, a member of one of the most privileged classes this world has ever seen. I was an educated American WASP (white, Anglo-Saxon, Protestant). It was my birthright to live a long and healthy life characterized by decency and good order. Theological adventuring was not on the agenda.

My religious community could have been summed up by the three Cs: confessional, conservative, cessationist. In short, we were absolutely sure our notions were right because they were cogently expressed in a written creed buttressed by ample scripture references. Second, we never made noise in public by taking politically charged positions even on social issues. And the deepest conviction of all held that the wild man of the Trinity, the Holy Spirit, had ceased to provoke the developed world and was off doing His thing somewhere else. We were now part of an advanced culture which could take care of itself without all the drama.

One of the most glaring examples of my spiritual myopia was the ease with which I breezed past Matthew chapter 10. Never once did I apply to myself the Lord's instructions to His disciples on the eve of their first swing through their home districts.

The Lord summarized for them evangelism 101. He said, "Heal the sick, cleanse lepers, cast out devils, raise the dead." I was certain this was not a literal directive for our day because the western world had the bases covered. The sick go to hospital and receive scientific care. Hansen's disease has been so completely eradicated or controlled that leprosariums closed long ago. The mentally disturbed are given counseling or drugs to hobble their inner demons. And the priesthood of science is hard at work on the challenge of cryopreserving corpses fully confident resurrection of the dead is just over the horizon. My faith community would allow the odd radical missionary from New Guinea to beat the air with his exhortations for heaven to come down and we might even believe his stories, but don't push it beyond entertainment around us.

The experiences related here could not possibly have occurred if Holy Spirit, our heaven-supplied prime mover, had folded His franchise and left us with only something in writing. These moments were clearly a blind side assault, a targeted confrontation. It was an exercise in both wonder and humility for which the educated, respectable normal I'd cultivated for 63 years left me completely unprepared. It was suggestive of so much more for which I had no grid. The unexpected result was to make the directives in Matthew chapter 10 plausible.

I was empty because playing church had become for me like paint ball combat. The parallel was real because I had played war once. I was taking cover behind a tree, convinced I knew where all the enemy were. Newbie that I was, early in the game I was winged in the arm by a paint ball from an unexpected angle. It left a yellow splash on my heavy jersey and disqualified me.

Unlike play war, however, this was no entertainment. When I was spirit-weary and without defenses I was met in a blind alley by a Presence who gave no name. God doesn't need a reason to interrupt our lives, only an opportunity. Since I chose to not back out of the alley, He found all the submission He needed.

I have no logical explanation for why these things occur. To humanity's endless question "Why?" the answer is always silence, a silence made deeper by the awareness that heaven's fellowship surpasses all understanding. My defense is that among the charismatic tribes where we have pitched our tent there is a high value for personal experience. There is a deference to what has been lived as told by those who are still alive, a delight in the Holy Spirit's life within us as shown by our many recent stories. As in the early New Testament church, a direct, personal encounter with the Holy Spirit fixes the context for public, corporate worship.

The Old Testament analogy is Moses in the desert calling out water from a boulder. God's written word is the rock, but the current stories one can tell of God moving in the life is the spring that flows from it. In shared experiences I found a living, drinking faith. It became a refreshment far beyond the arguments I had once received third hand, improbable doctrines based on selected Biblical passages, themselves derived from dialects no longer spoken and from times as strange to me as folklore.

It is important you know that among the charismatic tribes where we now worship the encounters you will read of here are unremarkable. They were certainly astonishing to me and what is now resident in memory has the bright quality of my first kiss. I haven't walked on water or seen blind eyes or deaf ears open at my touch or raised the dead. Yet. Others have, and if you take the time to find their stories and read without prejudice they are utterly believable. The sharp uniqueness of the moments when God touches you or works through you is the polar opposite of the monumental but lifeless logic of the doctrinal propositions about Him.

I have not written this testimony to shock or amuse for the wonders of the Kingdom of God are not a freak show or a fun house. However, to be drawn deeper into that mystery that leads us to a God who hides for us but not from us involves being stretched and challenged to the point of discomfort, again and again. You can't prepare for an encounter because God never does the same thing twice and in all the scripture I have never read that God apologizes. True, to test Moses, God repented once, offering to cancel the exodus and start over with His main man. So, plan B wasn't such a bad plan for Moses.

Some of what follows has been awkward to write, not because I regret anything I'm sharing but because so much of it is particular to time and circumstance. Other moments when the messages were for me alone, intimate as my own skin and precise as a scalpel, will remain in my journals.

Go back to the books of Hosea, Jeremiah, or Ezekiel and ask yourself if you could find the courage to share with even your closest friends, let alone unknown generations to come, the personal revelations you read there. When I consider the unprecedented sights that crashed in on them, their bizarre public behavior, and the threats to their lives following their damning, politically incorrect speeches I wonder what else we would find in their private journals. Even what made it to our day as holy writ strikes me often as awkward and gritty.

My comfort is that I have been transparent. Everything recounted here is as complete and as clearly stated as I know how and was captured within hours or at the most days of the encounters. My other comfort is realizing that the credibility of your own experience is not at risk here. St. Francis of Assisi was happy to be known as God's fool. It can't be any worse for me.

STEPS TOWARD
A FAR HORIZON

Make me know the way I should go. . .
lead me on level ground.
The 143rd Psalm

Though the same thought is attributed to several people, I read the following wry comment from Sophia Loren in the *Reader's Digest*: "Life is what happens while you're making other plans."

This reflection has a certain charm, a humble irony that takes the sting out of the memory of what we tried to do and failed. It's humanism at its best, but it's not the heart beat of what I read in scripture. The collection of the absurd (to those who don't believe) we call the Bible only happens to be the oldest and the most widely respected reference point for the inner meaning of life. What we see in those pages is the presence of Divinity working within human lives to transform randomness into destiny. What is unconnected when we walk alone blends into a narrative made sensible by Holy Spirit relating to us how much our life is valued by the higher world which calls to us.

My first step toward a far horizon was gaining a profound sense for 'home.'

I came into the world in November, 1944 to a mother living with relatives in New Jersey while my father was patching up soldiers in the European theater. I was never an Army brat because my father served only the time required of those whose medical school education had been subsidized by Uncle Sam. However, I do wear the smirk of a leading edge baby-boomer for I believe my conception was the main event during a furlough my father was given just before he shipped out to Europe. Though VE Day was May 8, 1945, there were so many thousands of GIs to bring home that he did not see me until I was almost a year old.

My father opened a medical practice in Brunswick, Maine after completing a surgical residency in Portland. We lived in town for a few years in a two-story brick house on Federal Street but most of my boyhood memories are of my idyllic life at Happy Acres. This was the name my folks gave to 27 acres of overgrown farmland in the

Pennellville district, a web of land four miles out of town between a stubby peninsula called Mere Point and the much longer peninsula of Harpswell Neck.

What has made this enclave a registered historical site are the several substantial homes built by the Pennell ship-building family. Over 80 sleek masted vessels were built during the 19th century not a mile from my home using timber cut from the woodlands I came to know so well. For the acreage and a down-at-the-mouth house/barn combo my parents paid $19,000 in 1951. If you have to ask what the properties are worth today you can't afford it, or the upkeep on large, 150 year-old post and beam houses perched on fieldstone foundations.

Some of my better stories are sprinkled throughout what follows, but what I could never adequately communicate is the enormous importance of a sense of place, a safe place that invites adventure. It was the supreme gift of those years and the bedrock on which a later and larger sense of home could be built. When the Spirit much later drafted me I already had a well-developed concept of safety and personal significance that immediately recognized the same at a new dimension.

I glory in the legacy of being a Mainer. I can not conceive

of a personal identity that does not include the face and smell of land. The trees become your trees, the sky reflects your emotions, the patterns of light and the color of the soil write a sacred text into your soul. In my case there was, in addition, the overlay of salt air, a distinct tang carried by every breeze. I spent so much time near and on the water that the rise and fall of the sea became an instinct. In summer I could predict the next tide to an accuracy of 15 minutes without ever consulting the tide tables.

An influence I did not properly recognize until late middle age was the spirit of great accomplishment that had hung in the air around me. Harriet Beecher Stowe, author of the explosive Civil War novel *Uncle Tom's Cabin*, lived and wrote the famous work three blocks from our first home on Federal Street. The campus of Bowdoin College, which saw so many students join the Union Army in the 1860s, was a block up the street from the Stowe House. Joshua Chamberlain had been a faculty member there and later was its president. Chamberlain led the defense of Little Round Top at the battle of Gettysburg. This desperate holding action leading a unit of Maine men was one of the two pivotal events at Gettysburg that ended the Confederacy's advance in Pennsylvania and turned the tide of war.

Whenever we went down Pennellville Road to the rocky beach on Middle Bay Cove we passed two magnificent homes. The larger one nearer the water had been built by the Pennell family patriarch, a fitting symbol of what was arguably the most prestigious American ship-building firm of the 19th century. Helen Keller spent several summers there. The one next to it was the long time home of Robert Peter Tristram Coffin who won the Pulitzer Prize for poetry in 1936. Our next door neighbor, Christopher Packard, was the curator of a museum and a published author of natural history.

I admired my father for his steadily growing success and influence but I never felt I had a claim on his attention. Instead, there were endless opportunities for outdoor play on thousands of acres where I had freedom to roam and on the sheltered waters of Middle Bay. This was more than enough for me to create my own world. My life was essentially self-directed. When out of the house my mother had only a vague notion that I was somewhere within a 2-3 mile radius.

Since my home life was secure I never knew anguish or a hunger for satisfaction. I studied the violin. I built model airplanes. I read every book on aviation in the Curtis Memorial Library, many while reclining on the sturdy limb of an apple tree. In late summer a snack was had by simply reaching up and picking a ripe apple. My reading tree stood next to the tiny, disheveled guest cabin with the rotting floor and sagging windows my sisters turned into their play house. I don't know how to even pray to be so carefree again.

I did the school thing. My grades were always good even though my mind was usually elsewhere. When it came time to choose a route into the adult world what was most clear to me was what I didn't want. I didn't want to be a doctor. If I had been given a word association test by a psychologist the first thing out of my mouth if he had said "Doctor" would have been "Absent." The science would have intrigued me and my SAT scores pointed clearly in that direction but there was no fire in the belly.

And there was Sheryl. Married while in medical school had a horrible reputation and waiting to be married for another four years after five years of courting was an unthinkable nightmare. A professional track nearly as attractive as medicine was the church, so I accepted a full ride scholarship to seminary determined to become a pastor. We were married the evening after Sheryl graduated from nursing school.

Seminary was a long parenthesis. It would have been the equivalent of holding my breath for two years except for adjusting to married life and the birth of our first child. Gratefully, Hebrew verb tenses and dull German theologians were eventually behind me and we were given our first pastoral assignment.

I loved the challenge of preaching and especially enjoyed the interaction with young people. I had short and uneventful ministry posts in Maine and New Hampshire. Scrambling to address emotional trauma, dysfunctional families, aborted theology, and local church politics is, of course, the very stuff of pastoral ministry. But I always felt this was prep work for something else, I just didn't know what. Compared to the stretching preaching brought me, these seemed like problems to solve instead of challenges to learn from.

The second step was becoming aware of the bottomless pit of human need, the darkness that shadows all of human history.

The church in our part of the country still held a traditional camp meeting – canvas tents, grass, common bathrooms, the whole sweaty summer catharsis. On a relaxed summer afternoon in 1972 a shadow passed

over our tent flap and a quiet bureaucrat from world
headquarters asked if he could talk to us. When he put
before us a request to teach in a bush secondary school
in Zaire I said Yes. I think Sheryl froze temporarily but
she was surely not going to let me go halfway around the
world alone.

A few of our experiences in Kasai province are told here
(today the country of which the Kasai is part is called
The Democratic Republic of Congo). You will read and
maybe try to pronounce the names – Lulengele, the
name of the mission; Mbulungu, the name of the village
just beyond the edge of our campus; Kananga, the city
50 miles away where we shopped – but you won't sense
the ache still in our hearts for that part of the world.

Africa engraved on me another sense of place, a world
where hope and opportunity are tentative, not expected.
I have burned on an inner eye the clusters of palm trees,
the sweep of waist-high grass and scrub bushes among
which human beings and their dwellings can hardly be
distinguished at any distance. A barely visible human
presence spoke volumes about unfulfilled potential and
the fatalism that were the undercurrent of tribal culture.

I learned to distinguish the regions men are from by the

smell of their ripe but honest sweat. I will never forget how rancid butter and flour spike the nose or the musky bloom of whole smoked monkeys hanging from the sides of heavily loaded commercial trucks. They were food for the travelers perched on top of the load 12 feet above ground.

And dinning still in my ear is the cacophony at night of insect noises beyond the window screens, nearly drowning out the muffled staccato of drums across the valley. Evenings were spent in the pool of light cast by a kerosene lamp, reading or listening to the BBC World Service on a battery-powered radio. These impressions are etched in the spirit as deeply as the traces of boyhood in Pennellville. The spirit of an entire continent lies there, huge, fierce, innocent, and sad.

But I was very happy in the Kasai. I faced challenges that stimulated me. Every practical thing I had ever learned was put to use. Surmounting the problems keeping a bush station operational often seemed more satisfying than directing the pastoral training school for which I was responsible. I arrived prepared to deal with practical issues, bringing with me the only complete set of tools on the station. I built a runway in the bush, repaired Land Rovers, designed buildings, including a work shop with an attached stores warehouse and a photographic dark room. I sourced supplies, supervised construction, and did my part to maintain the water system. Because we were on a station near the equator the length of the days was predictable but no two days' activities were the same.

I endured language bumps and scrapes teaching and preaching in French when, at least initially, some of my students had a better command of it even though it was their second language. The Zairois suffered my gaffes navigating the learning curve into their culture. There were uncertainties dealing with politicians and government agents. Cuban-trained Angolan rebels one time approached within 60 miles. For several weeks suitcases were packed and kept under the beds ready for a departure within minutes if necessary. There was even the disappointment of not being able to complete a full six-year term. We had to leave Lulengele because the physical demands and the tropical diseases had ground us down. Yet, despite knowing that everything done had been for the first time and then only half done, the memories are a treasury of simple joys, seeming greater in hindsight than the services rendered.

One night stands out above others. I had finished my

work in the large village of Bakwa-Tombe and was leaning back in a low-slung wicker chair. The sun had set and the stars seen through the palm fronds were thick and brilliant, a shimmering blanket covering me in splendor. I was surrounded by my African friends who plied me with ripe bananas picked that day and local peanuts warmed in the shell. There were only two or three small open fires for light. The soft conversation and quiet laughter made the utter blackness of the night a safer place than electric lights and walls can ever create for there was no 'outside' to threaten us. There was not a single reminder of the world I had come from. In a suspended moment, with affection I could receive but not then return, Africa quietly embraced me like a clumsy lover, and I did not resist.

The third step was learning the place of subtlety and surprise.

It's a difficult concept to convey because for so long I did not understand that the subtlety in which God moves is so much more profound than mere simplicity. Simplicity and integrity in life are visible qualities we all praise. But the Holy Spirit moves where we do not see Him. He is infinitely subtle, adopting any number of forms and voices and physical manifestations, never more than needed to support faith and never less than required to be certain of His presence.

Through many years of religious instruction and in my pastoral experience I became increasingly impressed that, with few exceptions, God's interventions in human history have been so subtle that unbelief has always been a rational option. It seems He has always opted for the fewest changes necessary to accomplish His purpose, always favoring the unseen forces that alter the dynamics of human life. Jesus himself suggested as much when explaining why he preferred to teach in parables instead of in the didactic form expected of teachers then and now. "So that seeing they may not see, and hearing they may not understand." Luke 8.10. He did not ridicule those who don't get it. There's no shame in it, just lost opportunity.

For centuries those few with a poignant and peculiar experience with God have been called mystics; not one of us, bizarre and unapproachable, perhaps even bent. In the long stretch of history there has been a bias for extreme economy in God's expression and scarce few voices to speak for Him, and those who did were rarely honored. I am grateful that today, at an increasing rate, a wider range of people with whom we can identify are

STEPS TOWARD A FAR HORIZON

now filling a prophetic office. But whether there are few or many voices, faith will always be required to look beyond the manner of presentation.

Review for a moment the evidence for subtlety. Creation is shrouded in eternal mystery since no one was present to file a dispatch. Moses saw a burning bush that was not consumed and which talked to him, but no one else did and we have to take his word for it. And, supreme example of all, the son of the most high God and co-creator of the universe was born in an animal shed, pushing through the birth canal toward the unknown like every other child, provoking not anthems of joy but rather birthing screams from his teenage mother and agonized hand-wringing by his father. Sure, the angels sang, the shepherds worshiped, and the magi appeared. But as Mary later shared these stories with his younger brothers they declined to believe that Yeshua was other than homely and human until after the resurrection . . . that defining event that, lest we forget, no one witnessed.

As a rural rabbi Yeshua bar Joseph healed hundreds as if it were a common thing. He did not ask for compensation from those delivered, so no rich man could ever boast that he had paid the highest price for his healing. He depreciated the temple system by restoring men and women without ritual and only rarely advised priestly confirmation as required by Torah. The anonymous and unsung simply stepped out of their painful normal into a new normal that was no more than parity with the normally functioning lives of those around them. The newly healed were not supermen. They would get sick again. Lazarus, if you can bear the truth, died twice.

It is not hard for me to understand why the keepers of power were not intimidated. The sensation of miracle moments was not transferable to those who had ultimate status to protect. In spite of the mass of circumstantial evidence surrounding Yeshua's ministry and the insistence of hundreds that their new normal was indeed miraculous, they killed him, anyway. In the absence of evidence they considered compelling it was simply the politically correct thing to do.

And if subtlety is typical of sacred history can we not expect the same of our own experience?

I began searching for the premises of a divine economy in the late 60s as I came to the end of my formal training. I became aware that the dynamics of a functioning utopia, a workable Kingdom of Heaven, had never so much as been suggested during eighteen years of church-sponsored education. That we were destined for a world without evil was a given. But exploring the parameters of a long term human experience somewhere in the cosmos was apparently a hobby left to science fiction writers.

In the summer of 1971, I accompanied my father on a trip to Georgia. His interest was an interview with the directors of Wildwood Sanitarium, a self-supporting health recovery enterprise. Unlike my father's plans for a community hospital in Brunswick, Maine, Wildwood's founder, David Frazee, had established the sanitarium to subsidize his religious commune. However, his ideas on holistic medical care had enjoyed success. On the return leg we also visited Little Creek School in Tennessee. This more rigorous, fundamentalist approach at the high school level stimulated my father's interest in alternative education.

It was probably on this trip that I began sensing a theme that had been playing in my spirit since my boyhood among the slow rhythms of field, forest, and tides. It would later develop into a conscious ethical and theological ideal – minimalism. I began to realize that the passion which has always moved me is to discover the root or core of things. A churning inside wanted to strip away the layers of propaganda and practice that clothed what I believed, to pursue the radiating light to its glowing filament though it blind me. I am Frodo Baggins and a simple ring enthralls me.

This construct of minimalism was encouraged by my father's conviction that the promise of heaven is a bonus. He believed there are many practical reasons here and now for being a Christian. But the economy of small, individual blessings was most dramatically reinforced from 1973-1977 during our service in Zaire. Certain images are still vivid.

SCENE 1.

My 6-cylinder Land Rover, Rattlin' Red Rosie, died on a trip to Kananga. It stroked out so suddenly for lack of a spark one might have thought a witch doctor had cursed it. I had seen the straw dolls on the side of the road pierced with needles to curse the occupant of a nearby hut. We had heard the stories of people dropping dead after a demonic curse. Why not a vehicle? (Though too naive to notice at the time, I later learned that, indeed, I had my enemies and critics among the Zairois.)

The highway to town, a mere dirt track, was now a workshop as I draped myself across the warm fender.

Traffic, should there be any, could simply go around, climbing either of the embankments that parallel all roads in that country. The embankments make the road a navigable ditch and are created by village road crews digging out the mud holes.

Diagnosis happily revealed a purely mechanical reason: a hairline crack finer than a spider's thread in the distributor cap – an absolute short circuit. Only one man could help me, the gruff German mechanic at the Protestant Center in Kananga. After hitching a ride on a passing truck, I frantically searched through two shoe boxes full of distributor caps and rotors he handed me. All of them were for the many 4-cylinder engines common to vehicles in the bush. Except for one 6-cylinder Land Rover distributor cap and one companion rotor. Without a word, just a wave of his hand, he gave them to me.

Now, there might have been an expatriate bush mechanic somewhere else in sub-Saharan Africa hoarding the needed cap and rotor. But it's not likely. Six-cylinder Land Rovers were exceedingly rare. Fearful that in case of a recurrence a second set would be unavailable, I might have been numbed with anxiety for the life forced on us, a life so foreign to the excesses of America, of scarcity even in essentials. Instead, there was that satisfaction one feels when a lock clicks shut, that shiver of certainty when the hammer releases and a rifle spits out a bullet. Beyond my whispered praise to God, seeing my unique demand meet its sole and adequate supply in an indifferent world had a symmetry no emotion could disturb. Men have made miracles of less. What no one else sees can change your world.

SCENE 2.

Kasonga, Sheryl's house boy and our quiet advocate in the village of Mbulungu, picking carefully through our waste basket to retrieve postal envelopes. He would slit them along three of the folds to recycle as writing paper.

SCENE 3.

At a piece work rate of about 25c per plant, a young boy from the village cleared scrub grass and created for us a plantation of pineapples. The vegetable gardening we were familiar with had been a failure. But the hardy pineapple plant, which can take root even when neglected, redeemed the worthless sandy soil to the south of our home. It was land too poor for anything but coarse grass on ground which sloped away gently at first, then pitched steeply into a jungly basin. Too far away, at the bottom of the tortuous trail to the bottom of the basin was rich soil and our water source.

Pineapples ripen over a long season, so my favorite fruit was fresh on the table a good part of the year. Kasonga would walk a few steps from the house and slap the thick stalk under a ripe pineapple with his machete. With a few strokes more to strip away the tough hide, breakfast was served. For 3-4 years a soil with no promise faithfully gave us golden gifts dripping with rich, stinging sweetness.

I am sure the plantation feeds the entire village to this day. Is their impromptu harvesting sharing or stealing from the family now living in the house we once occupied? It's an ethical question that no longer puzzles me as it once did. I have made peace with a culture that has minimal regard for private property. Since we had made forgotten land produce it never was a practical distinction in a culture based on hunting, gathering, and subsistence gardening.

SCENE 4.

My father was killed in an auto accident in New Jersey while we were stationed at Lulengele Mission. With the help of many friends, two ham radio operators, and advice from the State Department we were flown home within 72 hours of his death from half a world away.

On the way to my family home in Maine from JFK we stopped at a supermarket to buy snack food for the road. For long moments the sight of such plenty overpowered my intent to buy. My eyes struggled to find meaning among the options, a reason to reach for even a single item. I was numb with emotion and fatigue and there was no scarcity to prompt action. It was extravagance where simplicity was sorely needed. The shoppers must have been surprised to see a grown man wiping his eyes, sniffling and staring at the shelves, paralyzed by a surplus of choices.

On my writer's shelf of ideas there is a book I have yet to write. Its title will be *A Sufficient Paradise*. It's a work of fiction whose premise is a minimalist ideal for an earthly utopia. It will be my attempt to answer the following question: "If you could choose the fewest changes to the existing social order and physical environment that would produce a world you were willing to call Paradise, what would those changes be?"

Can we obtain the world our hopes confirm is real without cataclysm and spectacle? Would our present world, as now bracketed by maximum response

STEPS TOWARD A FAR HORIZON

to perceived foreign threats and zero tolerance of politically unapproved domestic behavior, accept such a minimalist premise? Or have we rather been blinded by flamboyant imaginations of heaven by evangelists or terrified by visions of apocalypse by novelists? Outside of the strictures of the Law, the children of Israel were not given detailed instructions for the rest of the society they were to build in the promised land, the only paradise they could conceive. Maybe my project is not only allowed but necessary.

The fourth step was to accept the wrenching truth that I had been discharged from one identity before receiving the next call that would define me. I had to be emptied. I would have to learn to walk in the dark and wait.

We returned permanently from Africa to a posting in South Dakota and faced crisis. Two crises, in fact. The first was to my health. Somewhere on a bush safari I had contracted microfilaria, a minute parasite that eventually takes up residence in every body fluid. At nearly the same time my mother contracted microfilaria in Tanzania while there on a short-term assignment with my father. In her case, the aqueous solution in the eye was so full of parasites the Tropical Medicine Clinic at The University of Toronto filmed the interior of her eyes. They had never seen such an advanced case in North America and wanted some video footage for teaching purposes.

Two to three months before leaving the Kasai I had become strangely lethargic in the afternoons. There was overall itching not accompanied by any rash. We passed off my condition as proof we needed a furlough, but The University of Toronto quickly diagnosed the real problem. The surprise treatment was a drug, Hetrazan, originally developed for veterinary medicine. For four weeks I laid on the carpet by the A/C vent in our South Dakota parsonage, too weak to turn over and unable to stand because of the crushing pressure in my skull, the side effect of the body expelling millions of tiny dead worms. Happily, the only lingering effect is the inability to donate blood. If you need practice dying this would be a fine beginner's exercise.

The second crisis was even more severe because it was within – something vital to my sense of self was in distress. I couldn't put my finger on it; I only knew I missed Africa. Not the scarcity, not the hardships, not the malaria and the chiggers. What I missed was the satisfaction of shaping a plan to meet a visible need and then seeing it immediately accomplished under my very hands or as the direct result of my orders.

A small plane we didn't recognize landed on the mission airstrip one day. From the passenger's side a confident young man jumped off the wing, an obviously well-educated young Zairois, with a cash box in his arms. He introduced himself as an agent of the American contractor building a power line across the country to supply electricity to the copper industry in Shaba Province. He asked if I would loan him a mission vehicle and a driver to deliver payroll to the contractor's camp nearby.

I was under a Land Rover fixing the brakes. Without pausing I called out to our driver, who was my go-fer at the moment, to use the other Land Rover and take the man with the money wherever he needed to go. The young man was surprised at my prompt response. Dropping his voice and thinking I didn't hear, he remarked to my driver, "Qu'il est expéditif, lui!" Translation – "He sure comes to a decision quickly!" See problem, speak the solution, done.

This marriage of freedom and responsibility in the face of the obvious had changed me more than I realized. Merely being employed was, quite literally, a world away from being needed. In my absence I could fill my pulpit in South Dakota with a phone call. But when it was time for the weekly two hours of electricity at Lulengele I was often the only one who could hand-crank the 3-cylinder diesel generator and light up the campus.

A dull ache that deep is not something I wished to process with the conference president who had just given a salaried pastor's job to a total stranger after reading his bio in a form letter. Neither did I wish to share myself with other pastors whose greatest problems seemed to be inadequate budgets and dwindling attendance. When the ministers in our district met quarterly I came home feeling like a hunted man. I had been emotionally drained by my furtive glances to determine if anyone noticed my discomfort.

As a clergyman should, I opened my Bible to find out what was backed up. I plumbed the Psalms without finding one that sounded like my soul's voice. I kept turning right in my Bible and skimmed my way through Isaiah. In the next to last chapter, number 65, I slowed down to savor Isaiah's rich imagery, the most magnificent prose in all scripture.

As he described our promised new heavens and new

earth my soul found its song. I was lifted above the moment; the ache was forgotten. Until I reached verse 22. A silent force met me there and I tightened inside.

"They shall not build and another inhabit." Something ominous began to race and slipped my grasp.

"For like the days of a tree shall the days of my people be." What was this! A sense of dread, the primal fear of falling was haunting me.

". . . and my chosen shall long enjoy the work of their hands."

At the word "hands" the dam broke. I sobbed like a child; great, wracking sobs. I couldn't stop. I could hardly catch my breath. My mind, so often the master of my moods, was offended and scolded me for allowing this loss of control. It made no difference. Twenty minutes later I finally regained my composure, wiped my eyes and finished the chapter.

A firm decision replaced the hurt which had drained away in the tears – leave pastoral ministry and do work I could see or allow a part of me to die. Something tangible must be demonstrated in a life of ministry or my spirit would not recognize it as genuine.

What followed was 28 years in business alternating between trucking and accounting. But directly out of this upheaval there grew unseen beneath the scramble of living a Spirit-fired conviction that charismatic ministry, where I could see power over nature with my own eyes, was a heritage I had been denied. In my education it was never respected, it was never modeled. Such risk-on ministry is the dynamic that made Yeshua untouchable even when He was defiantly inappropriate. Through it we plunder hell and advance the kingdom over ground that can be measured. It's the sharp edge of the axehead, the weighted point of the spear. I think it's what I'm supposed to do.

What I have found difficult to deal with is the urgency to share with others what can not be adequately described. A lingering preacher's duty demands more. Therefore, the best summary of the accounts to follow are the five lines that end *Peace Like A River*, the luminous novel by Leif Enger:

> Is there a single person on whom I can press belief?
> No sir.

All I can do is say, Here's how it went. Here's
what I saw.

I've been there and am going back.

Make of it what you will.

THE SUMMONS
JANUARY 2, 2008, EUCLID AVENUE

C.S. Lewis entitled his spiritual autobiography *Surprised By Joy.* Jack (as Lewis was known to his friends) had tried on each human philosophy as one would shop for the perfect pair of shoes, believing he would finally meet the God who harassed him at the end of a compelling argument. But it was the return of innocent joy, first known as a child, that startled and overtook him in the midst of successful middle age.

Beyond middle age a sudden longing overtook me, also. It was a trap laid by grace to snare my heart, to induct my spirit into fully responding to that love which admits no compromise and knows no fatigue. The Spirit broke through Lewis' last defense while he was riding to the zoo in the sidecar of his brother's motorcycle. As I should have expected from this and many other stories, the beginning of my adventure gave me no warning, either.

I was met by a surprise that transformed an irritation. But, I'm ahead of myself.

For the holidays, my daughter, Catherine, had invited her friends, Jonathan and Helena Cavan and their children, to spend some time with them in Acme, WA. They had all enjoyed the snow and the familiar rhythms of an American Christmas but it was now time to say good-bye.

Just before loading their bags into the rental car for the return to England Jonathan broke off the staid conversation one suffers through on such occasions and said to me, "Let me show you a website you need to check out." I showed him to my office on the ground floor. He sat down at the keyboard without comment and typed in 'ibethel.org.' When the home page was up, he arose with a curt, "Find out about these people," and left the room.

Writing today, I am so grateful to Jonathan. He lives in perpetuity as one of my online passwords. I praise God for a friend who sensed what I needed and didn't care what I thought of him. But, at that moment I felt a little put upon. First, he was an Englishman calling up the website of some American ministry or church I knew nothing about. And, second, after enjoying our hospitality for nearly a week he gave me no word of introduction or sense for why it was important to follow through.

I almost blew it off as a pretentious gesture from someone I had just beaten at the ping-pong table two evenings before. But I surfed the site and, just to cleanse my conscience of any hard feelings toward Jonathan, clicked on "The Sermon of the Week." It was Bill Johnson. I was incredulous, disarmed by such informed humility, alert to his uncommon grasp of the personal lives of Biblical characters, and charmed by his humorous prodding of the audience. Motionless, I listened to a voice of joy-based authority such as I had never heard before. It was a discovery as satisfying as a hot bath at the end of a cold day.

But in that moment the greater surprise was not the novelty of Johnson's delivery, unique as it was. I had heard well enough of good preachers in 60-plus years. I had spoken from a pulpit enough times myself not to be overly impressed by the eloquence of a man speaking to an audience trained not to interrupt. What was so sudden was the longing that gripped me. Shadows fled before a rush of light breaking in from another world. I saw lurking in my spirit where I had always feared to pry a waiting passion such as only mystics admit to, a hunger I had spent my life denying. Aroused by the light, emaciated passion and wheezing hunger stirred. I froze at their motion, knowing I could not return to the barren life behind me where my spirit did not thrive.

I had been diligent in the search for spiritual meaning and my teachers had given me willingly what they had. But I saw it now as so many desert years struggling alone up rocky slopes, slipping along narrow paths roughed out by theology. From the lower summits I was able to reach I had seen in every direction the high peaks that represent the heights of moral philosophy. Dramatic indeed were the thunder claps of doctrine and the rumblings of guilt and duty. But what I had never seen was a warm glow through the welcoming door and open windows of a home I would want to live in.

The wilderness time was not all wasted, however. I learned to guard my water holes, to cherish those witnesses who refresh me whenever I return. I learned the importance of good shoes, the scholarly habits that keep me moving over hard, uneven ground. And I hid behind big boulders when the sun blazed, sheltered by well-placed friends or the anonymity of the crowd during the heat of doctrinal wars.

When I was ordained to the Gospel ministry I thought I had signed a blank contract with God for Him to fill in at His leisure. It was for me to honor the terms of the contract through obedience to clerical officers. On that January morning I had long since stopped responding to a church hierarchy and I sensed that God had canceled my contract and would begin speaking directly. What might new drills and maneuvers look like when ordered by a voice more commanding than church loyalties?

When God began to challenge me by testing how much of Him I could bear it led to a lifestyle for which caution and compliance had not prepared me. When mystery leads you beyond yourself, what's next? That's what Abram asked when a naked Voice interrupted his settled pattern of success and said, "Leave all you know; you're a pilgrim until I tell you to stop." This first bewildered charismatic, with no sacred text to inform him or pastor to consult, did not even have a name for this Voice. The many gods of Haran he could hold in his hands. This God ambushed him from hiding.

The heart of any summons is to be called by name.

63

That's the essence of a subpoena which a process server is allowed to drop on the ground in front of anyone whose identity is verified. We all have jerked around to see who is being addressed when someone shouts, "Hey! You!" What did Abram do when his name was called? What would you do if the last shred of privacy was lifted by an audible voice you've never heard before but whose source you instantly recognize?*

ADDRESSSED BY NAME
OCTOBER 28, 2011, EUCLID AVENUE

I was curled up next to Sheryl at 6:45 AM, just below the awake level. She was asleep at that moment having a dream of herself praying with a group of women for healing from cancer.

I audibly heard my name spoken: "Dan." At this my mind was pinged and all the physical senses came to order. A second time, with greater clarity and volume, I heard my name spoken: "Dan!" There was no mistaking this voice; I had heard it before. It was distinctly female in timbre, and gave me comfort that the name I had

---

*A powerfully graphic presentation that shows Abram's perplexity can be seen in a 9-minute clip from the movie of his life by director Nyla Rossini. The entire 3-hour movie is available on youtube using this URL: youtube.com/watch?v=QHAL5SR1SXs. Begin at run time 0:20:53. The scene ends at run time 0:29:37.

picked for the Holy Spirit – Mariah – is not offensive to the Godhead.

I whispered, "I'm here, Lord. What do you want me to know?" Sadly, there was no more, only that refreshing flush that indicates the Spirit's presence. That flush which so much resembles a full-body response to a powerful magnetic field was repeated twice more, once with intensity, to assure me that this experience was not merely the play of my imagination.

THE BALANCE
MARCH 22, 2012, EUCLID AVENUE

Sheryl and I had been talking at the breakfast table about the examples of those who pray for the healing of total strangers they meet in public; while shopping or traveling, for instance. We had asked ourselves what the reasons were that keep us from doing the same.

Later in the morning we decided to walk to the bank together. While I am standing at the front door waiting for Sheryl the following is spoken into my spirit as clearly as casual conversation with a friend standing next to me:

"Your frustration when I do not move as you expect is matched by my disappointment when you do not do what I have asked you to do."

THE SUBMISSION THING
MARCH 23, 2012, EUCLID AVENUE

Sheryl and I parked the car at the downtown Bellingham terminus of the interurban trail that extends through Boulevard Park to Fairhaven. We paused before leaving the car to quiet ourselves and to confirm the presence of the Spirit before beginning the 5-mile hike that went through this heavily used public area.

As I prayed quietly to myself I felt an immediate resistance, involuntary but not unexpected, at the breaking of the day's rhythm. I repented immediately and asked, "Lord, why do I so quickly resist you?" The response followed as closely as the tail follows its dog, and it humbled me:

"It's because you have more practice resisting me than submitting to me."

NOTES FROM THE DARK SIDE

. . . the devil prowls around like a roaring lion,
seeking someone to devour.
I Peter 5.8

B efore we move into the light I want to shut the door on the dark side. The devil may stalk us, roaring like a hungry lion when he approaches, but when the heart is fixed on the Lord you love, a showman is all you're likely to deal with. He makes a lot of noise for someone who's defeated.

The believer has freedom to exercise authority when bullied by the powers of darkness. I once heard this from the Bethel pulpit: "We don't talk much about the devil around here. But when he crosses our path, we pull the trigger." Given the startling number of healings, signs, and wonders that occur at Bethel weekly the devils, apparently, are reduced to sniping and stay well clear, knowing the humiliation they would suffer if they showed up where no one is afraid of them.

For many years we attended Mars Hill church in Seattle. Their dynamic pastor, Mark Driscoll, once told this story from the pulpit. During an especially tense time quite early in the growth of their church a visitor began to manifest a demon spirit. He was subdued and the demon was summarily told to leave. Before he left, the demon tried to extract some sympathy by saying that he and his fellows were prevented from attacking the congregation. "Why do you say that," Driscoll asked. "Because," said the demon, "there is a dome that covers your building and we can't get in."

And the most dismissive response to an unwelcome presence I have ever read is attributed to Smith Wigglesworth, a man who is the nearest example I have found to a modern day Elijah. A man of such vigorous, aggressive faith, such astonishing intimacy with the power of the Kingdom of God was, as you would expect, a thorn in the devil's side. One night a demon woke him in his bedroom in the middle of the night. It was very possibly the crime boss himself, Lucifer, in view of the constant defeats they suffered from this man. The menacing spirit would have terrified me but Wigglesworth simply fixed him with a stare, said curtly,

"Oh, it's just you," and rolled over and went back to sleep.

There is no profit, only danger, taking the devil too seriously. My mother taught me this rhyme when I was just a boy:

> Sin is a creature of such frightful mien,
> To be hated needs but to be seen.
> But seen too oft, familiar with its face,
> We first endure, then pity, then embrace.

Long before I had unmistakeable and repeated personal awareness of intelligent beings in the spirit world I was the intended victim of what is best described as a spiritual hit-and-run attack.

The first of the two encounters in this short section comes from a time at the end of our eight-year stay in Lebanon, Oregon. During this period I had been involved in several businesses with only nominal and interrupted contacts with the church I had served as pastor and missionary during the 1970s. No observer at the time would have judged me an especially effective witness for the Kingdom of light and, in consequence, any significant threat to the dark side. Puzzling to this day is the nature and timing of the incident immediately following. I had the presence of mind to record it and discovered it 25 years later while sorting through a forgotten file.

WHITHOUT WARNING
FEBRUARY 19, 1988, HIDDEN VALLEY ROAD

At about 6:30 I was drifting through that strange zone between unconscious and fully awake. I was still aware of the last dream scene while becoming aware of the reality of my surroundings. Twice I heard the sound of forks, knives, and spoons being jingled together. It was very distinct; there was no question in my mind that the sound was coming from a point near my dresser and that the objects making the metallic clink were tableware.

To hear on these occasions of contact with the spirit world is difficult to describe and the verb 'to hear' is only an approximation. A sense for the distinction can be imagined in the experience of listening to music. We have all been in a room filled with audible sound, but through headphones the music seems inside us with no distance between us and it, more personal than hearing the same music projected into a room through speakers. Now, take the music analogy one step further and imagine sound impressions sent directly to the brain cortex. You would then be affected directly, all the sensations music inspires being experienced organically without the need for the ear to process sound waves and transfer the data to the brain. I can not think of a clearer analogy for 'hearing' in visions or in dreams than direct stimulus to the cortex.

I then heard a voice say, "I want you." The tone of voice was threatening, malevolent. It arrested and frightened me. Though I can not say I was terrified, I was concerned for my safety and began to pray in a confident rhythm, "Save me, Lord! Save me, Lord!" I felt vulnerable and, strangely, also a sense of awe in the presence of power I did not understand and could not control.

Gradually the sense of dread at the presence of evil so near me began to fade as I continued to rise to full consciousness. Now relaxed, I thought the encounter was over. Not so. While lying motionless on my stomach, and without touching or moving my blankets, the skin at the back of my head and down my shoulders and back to my waist began to tremble and quiver with goose bumps as if suddenly exposed to a sharp chill. It passed quickly but was dramatic enough to bring me fully awake.

71

Over the next two to three hours I felt an unusual sense of elation, a lightness of spirit that was almost giddy. It was a feeling deep within which did not interfere with preparing breakfast for the children or cleaning up the kitchen. The memory of this encounter with the spirit world has been amazingly clear, unlike other brushes with the paranormal that were quickly forgotten.

There is often an exquisite subtlety to Spirit/spirit contacts that is one of the strongest identifying characteristics. Many of the encounters I relate here occurred in The Zone, the place between sleep and awake when the spirit is especially vulnerable and sensitive. So important is this mode for communicating that the expression "Let me sleep on it" was coined by the early Quakers who cherished any opportunity for contact with the Holy Spirit.

THE TWO FACES
JULY, 2008, EUCLID AVENUE

I was sleeping soundly in the early morning hours when there appeared to me the head of a being, its face heavily shadowed inside a large hood or cowl. The visual impression was very like the evil emperor in the

NOTES FROM THE DARK SIDE

Star Wars films. It radiated elemental evil and I was terrified. I gave a sharp cry of fear. In an instant sleep left me and I was in a state above normal sleep but below full consciousness though I had heard my own startled voice. Sheryl later told me she heard me cry out but did not fully wake nor was she disturbed enough to elbow me.

I was struck by the graphic presentation of the shrouded head. It had the quality of a bold sketch on paper done in the heavy lines of a broad pencil and with great economy of line. A slight movement caught my eye that if continued would have illuminated more of the shadowed face, but to my immense relief the image dissolved before I saw the eyes or other principal features of a face. I prayed impulsively but silently, "Father, save me!" while the vision was fading.

Immediately there followed the vision of a second face, that of a full-maned lion. Think of the face of Aslan in the film version of the *Chronicles of Narnia* but done in the same bold sketch treatment of the first face. My heart leapt with the full, unrestrained joy of a child and it was as if I began running toward the lion without ever reaching him. The face radiated a fierce completed love, a warm wisdom and quiet assurance that banished instantly any fear ignited by the hooded figure of only a moment before.

It seemed as if images of all of life that is valuable were arranged in orderly ranks of dimmed lights to my left and right leading to the lion's face much as the walls of a corridor visually converge in the distance. The expression on the face was both a smile and a command and I would have thrown myself before the lion if I could have reached him. The vision faded quickly and left me very sad. I spent a good amount of time praising the Father for the gift of life and for the beauty of the lion and gradually fell back asleep.

One would expect that something so remarkable and memorable even in detail has a meaning, and so I believe. What remains now resident in the spirit is the assurance that though an enemy threatens me and would gladly sweep me away the Lion of the Tribe of Judah has the situation well in hand and will not allow my adversary to conquer. I also believe the experience was a benediction on my six months of study into the charismatic gifts and the supernatural activity we are invited to join, and that it was safe for me to continue my study until I found the place of the gifts in my own life.

This was not an experience one would ask for, yet, I will cherish it forever.

A NEW SET OF EYES

. . . the commandment of the Lord is pure,
enlightening the eyes.
The 19th Psalm

E very one, believer and nonbeliever alike, longs in his spirit to ascend to a high place, seeing far out and deep down, viewing with placid indifference the world's intricacy and charm from a sublime perspective. For the believer, the purpose would be to see the human experience from God's point of view and to praise Him. For the nonbeliever, the goal would be to measure the whole sweep of what man can grasp in order to praise himself. But the hope is the same – to see with a different set of eyes.

I had such a rare privilege one soft spring day in May, 1986. I had just been checked out in a Grumman American Tiger, a slick, 4-place private plane that handles like a sports car. Seeing my sister and brother-in-law in Pasco, Washington two hours away was excuse enough for my first cross country flight. I slid back the fighter plane-style canopy, buckled up, wheeled around smartly to the active runway (the Tiger has a castering nose wheel, like a grocery cart) and climbed out toward the Cascade range to the east of Corvallis, Oregon, my home airport.

The towering cumulus clouds already building in mid-morning like columns in a temple of the gods were my port of entry into a world apart only pilots know. I danced with one, then another, the clouds building faster than my little airplane could climb but always leaving me a corridor through which to advance heavenward. Then I was 'on top' for a few minutes, a solid cloud cover below me but seeing 'severe clear' in the weather ahead. At the ridge line of the Cascades the cloud undercover abruptly ended, its energy squeezed out of it as the air mass crested the dam of mountains and flowed into the Columbia River basin.

On the return flight late in the afternoon I was expecting magic. I was not disappointed. Through the day strong convective activity east of the Cascades had built a cloud barrier in front of me that forced me higher and higher. The throttle was pushed to the firewall as I climbed through 10,000 feet. The engine gave all it had left in the thin air, struggling now with less than half of the 180 horsepower I had taken off with near sea level in Corvallis. And still the clouds challenged me.

I passed 12,000 feet, the level above which Federal Air Regulations require the pilot to begin breathing oxygen. I didn't have any. But, since I had been enjoying a God's eye-view of our planet during this flight I felt God would understand if I gave myself permission to bend the rules. I eased through 13,000 feet just as the last clouds retreated behind me at the Cascade crest when I passed over a saddle between mountains. Looking down and to my right I watched the skiers near the top of 11,240 foot Mt. Hood. On probably their last run of the day the skiers sashayed in slow motion, reluctant that their play day on the slopes should end.

It was my first time to look down on the top of a snow-covered mountain from an aerial perch where I was pilot-in-command. I felt myself the master of all I surveyed. The Cascade range stood away to the south, one aloof peak after another. The tip of Mt. Hood and Timberline Lodge were my footstools to the right, and the silvered Columbia River 25 miles away framed my world to the north. The low coast range, 80 miles away in front of me to the west, was already marching its shadow across the Willamette River Valley while the wisps of cloud around their stooped heads were fast fading to pink and peach. I felt that no one could resist loving such a beautiful world, that the problems humans create are hardly to be mentioned in the face of such imperturbable majesty. I was enchanted.

I banked gently to the southwest where 115 miles away I could just make out the winking green and white beacon at Corvallis, the welcome sign of an open civilian airfield. I trimmed the nose down and reduced power for the longest toboggan ride of my life. The Tiger quickly picked up speed until the needle went past 200 MPH. This was beyond the 'never exceed' speed (Vne) of the airframe, but in the evening air there was not a ripple. It was as smooth as oil on silk and I felt confident that my second rules infraction of the day would also go unpunished.

True to the quick calculation I had made when passing Mt. Hood, in less than 35 minutes and at exactly the pattern altitude (800 feet above ground) I reached the boundary of the airport traffic area. Relishing the memory of the long slide out of the mountain heights made me sit up straighter. I hung out the flaps and throttled back to a slow approach speed of 65 MPH, unwilling for my day to end.

Then there was the turn to final approach; in a quarter mile the magic would end in the falling light. With a sigh I slipped from the hem of the velvet sky and kissed the earth with my wheels, alive from the briefest whisper I had heard of how much we and our planet are loved.

I think you will understand from the following encounters how the whimsy, humor, and affection of the Holy Spirit has allowed me to view the Kingdom of God with a new set of eyes.

THE BROKEN STEERING WHEEL
JUNE 18, 2010, McLEOD ROAD

Sometime around 4:00 AM, while in the neutral zone between sleeping and waking, I was aware of a faint, fading sequence of impressions that represented life's desires. These were the normal, healthy appetites for food and for intimacy, the dreams of what home to live in, what car to drive, etc. These are the gifts the heart that is loved recognizes, the things we reach for and for which we need never repent.

Against a background of light, of indistinct and gauzy images that glowed and then faded, there appeared a very distinct image of a steering wheel. It was turning clockwise and continued slowly to rotate without stopping.

Since at the time I was driving a truck for a living, when the steering wheel did not stop after several complete turns I realized with a start that it was broken. Without reflecting, my soul rose and asked, "Lord, are you telling me you want to steer?" Instantly, I heard the words, "I will steer."

This was not amorphous thought but distinct words, yet the expression was without sound. Compared to the larger urgency of my question the response was like the smaller type of a footnote at the bottom of a page.

This is my interpretation of a very singular event. There is a time coming when dreams and desires of all kinds, all of them healthy and normal, can be pursued. The vision was a warning to me that by myself I can not steer successfully through this field of opportunity and that my Lord expects me to trust Him to navigate. When the steering wheel appears broken He can still direct.

THE GATHERING
NOVEMBER 21, 2010, McLEOD ROAD

"Is The Arm Of The Lord Shortened?"

We were worshiping with The Gathering, the name for our small house church. We had a marvelous time sharing those portions of scripture that had become a campground for our spirits during times of trial and triumph, verses or passages that had lifted off the page and spoken directly to each of us.

We then filled our bowls and plates with the potluck meal we always shared and took our seats around the dining room table. For reasons I forget, I was sharing with the group my visit some years before to a tailor in Los Angeles. I had always wanted a custom shirt maker to take exact measurements that would take into account the fact that my right arm has always been an inch shorter than my left arm. I then extended my two arms full length and compared them. The asymmetry was obvious to everyone.

I was sitting at one end of the long table. Deborah Roberts was sitting to my right and Sheryl was sitting to my left. Deborah had stopped eating while I was describing my anomaly and she caught my eye and asked with complete sincerity whether I wanted my left arm shorter or my right arm longer. Confused by her directness and what I thought was the irrelevance of the question, I finally stammered that longer was better than shorter and I would choose to have the right arm grow. This oddity had never been a problem, not even remotely a handicap. My private thought was that Deborah was being solicitous, remembering a recent kindness to her that had been my pleasure to perform.

I went back to my food and the conversation picked up where it had paused. Quietly, Deborah said, "I command this arm to grow and match the left arm." I stopped eating and looked at her, surprised that her prior question had been the setup for this demand on the Spirit springing from her faith, a faith that, frankly, I did not share. My private thought was, "How sweet of her to want such a thing for me. How like her spirit to be generous. I hope she'll not be disappointed as this is not a problem which needs fixing." And I returned to my food.

At that moment I was 'tapped' in my spirit and directed to acknowledge that when she had spoken I had simultaneously felt a soft, warm brush on my right forearm as light as a feather's stroke that began just below my elbow and lifted short of my wrist. The sensation was so subtle that it was an act of faith to receive it and a second act of faith to declare it. But I did acknowledge it, though only to myself to consider later when the strangeness of the situation was past.

Deborah was insistent. "Stretch out your arms again and let's see what's happened." I did. My right arm was now exactly the same length as my left arm. It still is to this day.

Sheryl burst out, "They're the same length!" I was dumbstruck, motionless temporarily by a change I, of all people, could not possibly deny. Then both Sheryl and Deborah erupted in laughter, saying, "You should have seen your face!" The table conversation was interrupted for a few minutes while everyone joined in the wonder at what a playful Jehovah had just done. Papa God must have been laughing, enjoying a sacred mischief that bursts from the same simple joy we all know when springing a surprise on our children. And then we finished our meal, albeit at a higher level of excitement and satisfaction that heaven had briefly touched earth and we had been given the honor of seeing it.

SHARING THE WONDER
NOVEMBER 21, 2010, TACOMA

That same evening we attended a healing conference in Tacoma. Our particular interest was to hear the remarkable prophetic voices of Randy Clark and Georgian Banov. We had first learned of Bulgarian-born Banov in the movie *The Finger of God* where his outrageous joy in the Lord's service was one of the highlights and set for us a new boundary for appropriate expression. Randy Clark was known to us through his long-time relationship with Bill Johnson and their partnership teaching in healing conferences around the world.

At the end of an exalted worship time, and having taught us the fundamentals of supernatural gifting, Randy Clark entered a period of intercession for healing. One of the specific conditions for which he said the Lord desires to show Himself superior is through canceling the presence or effect of metal in people's bodies as a result of surgery. He has seen plates, screws, and rods either become plastic as a result of divine healing or completely disappear. And miracles already released that result in testimony can become a legal precedent that the Lord honors with an additional release of the same type of healing miracle.

Sheryl had had reconstructive surgery on the big toe of both feet about 18 months prior. The procedure leaves behind two small titanium screws in each toe that fix the resectioned bone in place. While she had regained about 80% of full function and was able to exercise with only slight changes to her routine there was frequent residual pain in her left foot and her right big toe would not curl downward completely so as to touch the floor and assist with balance.

While Randy Clark was still speaking and before specific prayer was offered to address the many situations represented by raised hands Sheryl became aware that the persistent pain in her left foot was gone, completely. Intrigued, she removed her right shoe and realized that her big toe now responded normally and made solid contact with the floor. When invited to bring a testimony she went quickly to the front and had the joy of sharing a hallelujah report with everyone.

Since then there has been virtually no pain in the left foot (ill-fitting shoes will provoke the area) and the right big toe still functions through its full range. Two weeks later at a healing service conducted by Georgian Banov

Sheryl testified of her experience and the permanence of the change.

How is it possible for your heart not to be captivated by such extravagant, hilarious blessing as we had seen on this day? Never will I be able to forget that God's agent on earth, the Holy Spirit, has an infectious and unpredictable sense of humor blended with that astonishing grace to never diminish us which is the hallmark of the Kingdom of God.

WALKING THE COSMOS
MAY 13, 2011, BELLINGHAM - AT STUDY

Friday night prayer and study at Hunts. The DVD presentation was by Judy Franklin to the first-year students at the Bethel School of Supernatural Ministry. The subject: seeing Jesus while spiritually present in the 3rd heaven, an exercise with which she is so familiar that one wonders if, like Enoch, she simply doesn't show up at work one day because her return ticket to earth was canceled. She asked the class to close their eyes and let a picture of Jesus present itself. We who were watching the DVD did the same.

What I saw – A figure defined by shades of gray was standing in front of me. The figure was muted as if standing behind a very fine sheer veil. The figure was Jesus. He was magnificent even in shades of gray, His form and clothing muted by the veil between. He had the strong, masculine beauty of a young Sean Connery, the tall, spare, aristocratic carriage of Richard Chamberlain, and the suppressed humor and common sense of Ronald Reagan in his prime as President. I could only stare, speechless at such glory in human form.

What He said – "Go and grow. The more you grow the more magnificent I become."

Where He took me – Together we went for a stroll through the cosmos, me just a half-step behind and to His right. We walked, we did not fly. We walked past solar systems within the background galaxies. Time condensed, and after what had to have been a long walk we came upon an empty planet in an unknown solar system. Our pace slowed until we could step on to the planet much as one steps on to dry land after a ferry ride.

The surface of the planet was absolutely barren, like the surface of the moon or of Mars. He turned to me and said, "This planet is for you to build a world with. I will teach you how to create with words." And then, with a slow, warm smile, He added, "But, take your time."

A VISION OF FATHER'S SECRET
OCTOBER 29, 2011, BELLINGHAM - AT REST

We were with Bill and Linda Boone, hearing their stories of learning to 'soak' in the Presence and how to lead others to experience the same thing. I related the following vision which I had received during the soaking session they had hosted.

I saw a dam in front of me made of layer on layer of discards, tier on tier of clutter. Behind this accumulation of disposable, lifeless objects, this vast junk yard of used up and thrown away ideas or possessions, I was aware of something full of life that was rising rapidly. When it appeared above the topmost layer of rubble I saw a large face in profile – the face of Father. He was laughing so uproariously He was almost shouting. His complexion was as ruddy as warm bronze and He had an unruly mass of curly hair.

A moment later I was aware of Him looking straight at me. Words fail to describe the expression. What

90

came to mind were the words of Jeremy Riddle's song; "His love is fierce, His love is strong, it is furious." The response I felt was "the fear of the Lord," the fear of ever depending on anything else, the fear that desire might cool until I could be satisfied with anything less. One feels exposed but without any impulse to hide, naked but without shame.

I then perceived how He views me. From His perspective I am a piece of artwork, intricate, wholly original, but alive and growing. Like much modern artwork I have seen, the sculpted piece was not solid. There were many voids or spaces in this piece of artwork that was me. Before He fixed his gaze on me the spaces were all filled with material that is not eternal and did not originate with Father's design. His presence was so strong that, like light so powerful it becomes a warm breeze, everything of this earth or of my own invention that filled these spaces was simply blown away. What was left was incredible, astonishing artwork of whimsy and divine genius that could never be duplicated.

Then I understood the reason why we have so many voids and spaces in our heaven-created self. It is so that God may enjoy us by breathing and shining through and around his artwork. He does not merely see or touch us.

He experiences us, and He allows us to also experience ourselves as He does when His life flows through and around us.

Here is the anomaly, though. To all others who see us (from behind, so to speak) we appear solid and whole. Others can relate to us but no one but Father can experience us completely. There is, therefore, an inviolable privacy which guarantees permanent significance. Father will never part with any of His artwork.

The following is attributed to Mahesh Chavda:

"On earth those who have a great revelation are honored. But in heaven we are known by the secrets we keep; what is known only between the Self and Father."

CROSSING
FRONTIERS

Let us go up at once and occupy it,
for we are well able to overcome it.

Numbers 13.30

During the second world war my father was a
surgeon with a mobile army surgical hospital (a
MASH unit) following a few miles behind the troops
as they pushed back the Germans from the Normandy
beaches. He brought back his share of souvenirs
including a German military policeman's aluminum
foot locker we still use today and an ornate dagger and
scabbard, its handle decorated with an inlaid swastika.

When I was about nine I found these items when I
was poking around one idle summer day in the attic
of our home on Federal Street. I turned my head and,
standing in a dark corner, what to the eyes of a boy was
the grand prize, I saw a .22 caliber rifle. Eureka! When
I asked boldly if I could have it, my father explained that

when he found it in the cellar of a bombed-out house he had determined to bring it back for the son born in his absence. But I could only remove it from the attic and call it my own when I was twelve and old enough to handle it. And I could fire it only when he was home.

Before I was twelve we moved to Pennellville. Here there was plenty of room for me to target practice on our own property and I looked forward eagerly to my twelfth birthday. True to his word, on my big day I was given the rifle with the repeated condition that I could shoot only when he was present. A busy surgeon burdened with the additional responsibility of overseeing the health of the hospital he had helped build does not have much time to spend in leisure pursuits at home, so I went plinking behind the barn at cans perched on fence posts only once or twice.

One day the following spring, without comment or seeking permission from my father, I determined to solve this annoying problem by myself. I felt for the first time in my life the freedoms of an adult. I owned a gun, didn't I? So, I hid the rifle on the floor behind the front seat of my father's car when I rode into town with him for his patient appointments. As soon as he was occupied I retrieved the .22 and walked the one block to Maine Street, turned right toward the Firestone store, and proceeded with a determined stride through the business district of our town carrying the rifle in full view of the traffic in the street and the pedestrians on the sidewalk. I was oblivious to the stares, but I must have been quite a sight. The consequences to a 12 year-old boy doing the same today are too grim to imagine.

I strode into the Firestone store. Without explanation I set the rifle on top of the glass display case and asked the clerk if he would trade me straight across for a Daisy BB gun. There was a short pause while the clerk got his bearings, then he reached behind him for one of the BB guns in stock and the deal was done.

To my father's eternal credit he never said a word in reproach when I told him at supper what I'd done, though the expression on his face told me clearly I had crossed a frontier and was now in uncharted territory. He had, in fact, given me the gun as a gift and I was free to do with it as I pleased, but a shift had occurred and our relationship changed that day. I had, in fact, made a bad trade in my haste (air pressure is a poor substitute for gun powder) but solving a problem on my own was all gain.

Crossing spiritual frontiers is the same. We never need to ask permission to make progress and initial judgments may be a mistake. Passion leads and the boundaries crossed are seen best in hindsight.

A second thing I learned from this incident is that wherever you grow, someone else made a way. This lesson was reinforced for me some twenty years later. I learned that at the time of my march down Maine Street, without knowing it, I was living in the shadow of my father's reputation.

Here's the rest of the story. I have referred elsewhere in this account to my father's tragic death. I had the honor of being asked to preach his funeral sermon. I was, mercifully, too numb with grief to be intimidated. I remember only the last few words of my conclusion but little else of the proceedings.

After the service I rode in the limousine as the long procession of cars wound its way down Maine Street on its way to Riverside Cemetery. At the turn to Pleasant Street there was the usual police courtesy traffic control. I was struck by the sight of an older gentleman I later learned was a retired sergeant from the Brunswick Police Department who had volunteered for duty that day. He was standing at attention in his dress uniform, saluting the passing casket while tears streamed down his face. He had been one of my father's patients and, like so many others, had loved my father honestly, beyond the professional respect in which he was held by all.

Now, return to the scene of me at 12 years-old walking down that same street with a firearm in full view. This same sergeant was on duty that day working the opposite side of the street. Alerted to the unusual sight, he was about to cross the street and apprehend me when he recognized who I was. "That's Doc Bettle's boy," he had said to himself. "He's OK. Not to worry."

LAURIE NEWTON
LATE 2008 – SUMMER 2010

Sometime after our odyssey began, an urging followed by reminders began to repeat itself in my spirit. It was a call to pray for a friend and colleague Sheryl had met while working at Skagit Valley Hospital. I dismissed it as a random thought prompted by Sheryl's telling me of Laurie's many struggles with deteriorating health.

But the thought kept returning, always with a raised

sense of urgency. So I took it on as a prayer project much as one goes to the gym to tone the muscles and quiet the voice of conscience. I had been reading the testimonies of divine healing for months so why not act as if it could be true for someone who was now, apparently, my responsibility?

Whenever I was prompted I would pray for Laurie Newton to be healed. I am sure I prayed for her nearly every day for some months. I was never too specific. She had enough ailments. God could take His pick and start anywhere.

In May, 2010 she was admitted to hospital with a potentially life-threatening pulmonary embolism. It was touch and go for about 36 hours. My prayers for her, now well-rehearsed, were brought to combat readiness and I contended with confidence for her life.

When the crisis passed her physician sat beside her bed and calmly told her she should be dead. At a follow-up exam a month later the exam notes read:

"Pulmonary arteries are normal in size, and demonstrate no intraluminal filling defects to suggest central pulmonary embolism. Previously seen saddle pulmonary embolus and segmental pulmonary emboli have resolved."

Shortly after the crisis, and after having seen the alarming CT scan taken on her admission to the hospital, Laurie wrote me the following email:

"I slept long and hard last night and got up this morning feeling different. When the fog cleared, God had a message for me. . . He told me I am alive only because He 'commissioned' you to pray for me and cover me and you were obedient. Your obedience has been long lasting and complete. You spiritually have my back which is my long standing plea and heartache . . I believe because of my personal story that God needed to give me tangible proof of your commitment in prayer for me."

Semper Fidelis. It is not a boast. Every Marine knows it is an ideal and a command.

ONE – AND BY ONE – IN THE SPIRIT
SEPTEMBER 8-11, 2010, SPOKANE

To the 12th annual general meeting of the International Association of Healing Rooms Sheryl and I had the

pleasure of sharing a ride with two new friends, Doug and
Sandy Bryan. It was seven hours in a rich mix of hilarity,
holy tears, and memories of lives blessed and now gifted
to each other. We saw the high bluffs of open range land
above the Columbia River where Sandy had earned her
college tuition rounding up cattle on horseback. We
passed the Gorge, the site of the amphitheater along the
Columbia where our friends, then a much younger and
more daring couple, had once attended a rock concert.
They had left before the concert ended because, though
not toking a joint themselves, they were already half-
stoned from the thick clouds of pungent Mary Jane
smoke. It was a road trip to remember.

The IAHR that year had passed a millennial milestone
when the 1000th healing room opened . . . somewhere.
It's hard to keep track of an organization this dynamic,
that is so focused on service to others and not on its own
record. Before the year was out there would be another
1000 healing rooms just in India. The necessary cadres
in that vast country had already been trained and that
November a mass investiture had been planned. In
one stroke there would be a doubling of people serving
and broken people being served. So urgent are the
practitioners that many of the 'healing rooms' in India
are simply an agreed upon place to meet in the shade

of a tree. Even a shouted Hallelujah is a weak response to such a vast impulse to intercede and see men whole. Hallelujah, none the less.

Sheryl and I were the amateurs, the newbies with only a few months of healing rooms team experience in Bellingham. And added to that, this would be the first time we would ever worship and learn in a large company of avowed charismatics. The old prejudices lingered just outside the foul lines in full anticipation of our disapproval and discomfort watching 'holy rollers' put on a show of self-induced euphoria.

The story in short: it never happened. Two people raised as we had been in a very different tribe of Christians could not have been more surprised or more gladly welcomed than we were. Far from frantic, the overall tenor was a joyful calm, the most exceptional sight being that of a cluster of two to five gathered around another, contending for a desired breakthrough. For a companion view of such a transition from skepticism to participation I encourage you to find and read the classic in this field, a marvelous story by John Sherrill entitled *They Speak With Other Tongues*. In print since 1964 and having sold over 2.5 million copies you will probably find it in paperback in your favorite used book store. I did. Three copies at $1 each.

What would I most want you to have shared? That's easy – the music! To experience music as a continuous, seamless foundation for both corporate and individual worship is to be not just lifted above the mundane and vexing but to be suspended in an atmosphere where an expectation of blessing is as natural as breathing.

I timed the worship service. It was 50 minutes from Don Potter's first chord riff until we all reluctantly made ready for a mere human to talk to us. In that time the music never died. It swelled to the climax of the song being given (as opposed to performed) and then in a natural diminuendo as sweet as the sigh of a lover it would fall to a whisper. A simple, quiet chord was held by the keyboardist with only the most gentle improvisation, the drummer brushing the cymbal to keep the music awake. And then the vocalist, or Don Potter with his guitar, would sing a hymn invented in the moment as our gift to the Spirit, that steward of the Kingdom who held us all in a quiet more active than silence, in an attitude of worship richer than thought. I would go back there in a heartbeat.

So far, Sheryl and I were not completely alien to the

experience of those around us. In touring choirs we had ourselves sung sacred concerts of more than an hour with only brief, silent intervals between the pieces on the program.

But then we became caught up in congregational 'singing in the spirit' that took us completely by surprise. At the end of the Thursday evening presentation, in an atmosphere of serenity and holiness, the speaker started a simple chorus. At the end, and having sung it through only twice, the music would not leave. On the same chord with which the previous chorus had ended the audience lost itself in worship. Softly, hundreds began to sing in tongues, or what we have now learned is more proper to call one's prayer language. The chord held, swelling and falling with a life of its own, a tidal rhythm of spiritual presence. No one was directing and no one cared to. It was electric. By resting on one chord it was musically shallow, but it was too rich a symphony of worship to describe by anything we had ever known.

Twice more during our four days together the same occurred, lasting as long as 10 minutes. Credible witnesses, fellow team members at the healing rooms, told of other conferences where singing in the spirit was joined by heavenly voices with vocal ranges far beyond anything humans can reach. Oh, to sing with the angels!

The worship leaders were Don and Christine Potter. He sings and plays guitar and she dances behind him as an expression of the music. That may sound like high school amateur night until I tell you more about Don Potter. He is one of the most respected arrangers and producers in Nashville where he has been the genius behind the sound of many of country music's headliners. He is widely credited with creating the unique Wynonna Judd sound. A very partial list of others for whom he has been a recording producer would include: Tricia Yearwood, Kenny Chesney, Willie Nelson, Dolly Parton, Toby Keith, and Clint Black. These names are just for the flavor; the list is very long with names everyone knows. After 40 years in the music business he is known and valued everywhere. However, if you go to his website you will only find his worship music for the real joy in his life is to bring others into the presence of God.

Some, more uninhibited than I am, needed to move and dance. For them, there is flagging. There were many flags, beautiful translucent silk creations in a profusion of colors and designs made available to all for worship by the flag vendor. Once, I counted. The seating area for 3000 was surrounded by flags, 40 or 50, held by those who wished to express their worship in motion and color. The flag carriers would gather in a circle and raise and lower their standards in unison. Later, they would form a line and jog slowly down the aisles and across the auditorium behind the stage from which the musicians maintained the musical foundation for worship. The colors rippled and as they passed those of us seated on the aisles felt the breeze. Sometimes the carriers dipped their colors to skim lightly over the heads of those who, heads and hands lifted, smiled at the soft symbol of the Spirit's presence. The flagging continued in utter silence to let the music have all our voices while they held all our eyes.

Children, one as young as 2 or 2½, her diaper bouncing, loved the flags. Some flags were sized for little people and they would walk among the adults or skip along freely, alone or in twos and threes. They didn't laugh or chatter. They felt themselves part of the worship and recognized the spirit in the room. Not once in the four days did any of the many children present disrupt the event by crying out.

One young man, holding the white and blue-barred flag of the State of Israel, worshiped alone in a far corner of the auditorium where a bright mercury vapor lamp created a dramatic pool of light. After waving it above his head in slow circles in silent harmony with the vocalist he stretched himself full length upon the polished concrete floor. The long corner of the erect flag rested on the small of his back while he prayed for God's mercy to remain with His chosen people. "Pray for the peace of Jerusalem." I was deeply moved.

There is too much for me to remember without aching with nostalgia. Worship, one speaker said, is the only thing we do in groups that prompts heaven to show up. Whatever truth might be spoken in a sermon could not express anything not long ago known. But worship is ever new. Another said, laughing, "Try to enjoy it; this is only choir practice for our principal occupation in heaven." We all left with regret, returning to the management of our lives but infected with the enthusiasm of insurgents determined to invade the world when and where it does not expect us.

At 5:30 AM on the last day I awoke with a song being sung in my spirit. I distinctly heard both words and melody. Groggy and fumbling in the dark, I got up and wrote it down. Ten minutes working in the bathroom and I had the first draft. Perhaps it's a poem. If so, it is more in the manner of an English-translated psalm where the balance is in the thought structure.

YOU ARE MY PORTION

You are my portion in this life,
My sole provision all of my days.
The closer to you the more I desire
To follow your Spirit and learn of Your ways.

Chorus:
"So sing all the earth!" rings the voice from the
  throne;
"I sent you my Son to love as your own."

You guard my soul, angels stand watch
Around me in strength, a wall against pain.
You build me up when others tear down;
My joy is Your trophy and You are my gain.

Chorus:
"So sing all the earth!" rings the voice from the
  throne;
"My Son gave His life to make you His own."

Now the rivers run full, the springs swell with praise;
New wine and new oil flow freely to all.
The harvest is in, we've washed at the well,
The supper is ready, we've come at Your call.

Chorus:
"So sing all the earth!" rings the voice from the
  throne,
"Rejoice as my Son claims you for His own."

OPEN HEAVENS
OCTOBER 13-15, 2010, BETHEL

Returning from a visit with family in Southern California we had the enormous blessing of attending an entire conference at Bethel Church in Redding, CA.

How do I describe what it feels like to be stretched and stretched again? It is to move forward cautiously with a step taken in fear, then a next step of a building faith joining the momentum around you. Continue, and the soul and spirit cry for home while the world fades, gray and weary.

Three things stand out from our three days at the conference. The first is the security of being in an atmosphere that shelters and serves you. One feels that worship and training others to enter the spiritual territory they have colonized is in fact ALL that Bethel does. They live for this, they organize for it. It is so powerful a force that any call for loyalty would be superfluous. In modesty, the leadership at Bethel speaks only of a culture they have nurtured, but it is more than that. They have created a dwelling place where the Spirit is welcome. We felt we had found what is at the heart of the concept of sanctuary.

The second note that still sounds these years later is the memory of having been the target of prophecy. We had purchased coffee from HeBrews, the delightful name for the coffee bar in the lobby, and were seated on the open air patio enjoying the soft evening air and the view of Mt. Shasta. Two young men were at the next table unpacking a new camera one of them had purchased. After a few minutes the new camera owner left, but his friend lingered a few moments as if in thought. Rising to leave, he went about three paces, just beyond my peripheral vision, and stopped. Approaching from out of sight, the next thing I knew a hand was on my left shoulder. "The Lord gave me a word for you. May I sit down and tell you what He has for you?" a voice said.

Though startled, I said, "Of course! But make sure you give us all of it." And then followed ten or fifteen uninterrupted minutes of prophecy over our lives flowing from an awareness of who we were, an awareness that could not have been divined from ordinary human contact as the young man was a complete and utter stranger to us. While helping his friend unpack the camera only three feet from us he, nevertheless, had appeared oblivious to our presence and neither he nor either of us had spoken. The apt words for both of us and the coincidence of events left a powerful impression on us both. Two days later I saw him on a sidewalk from a distance so I know he was flesh and blood.

The last thing I want to recall is difficult to share and harder to describe. I prayed in tongues for the first time. The experience is difficult to share because it was and remains intensely personal. Those who make a public display of this gift violate its nature. As the apostle Paul instructed the believers in Corinth, the gift of tongues is uniquely for personal edification and when it disrupts a public service is to be interpreted or the speaker must refrain.

Since the gift of tongues is to be desired I had been praying for the experience, and though others had prayed over me and added their faith to my desire, it had been without success. I had come to Bethel with some hope for a breakthrough, however. When a friend had laid hands on me and prayed for me one Sunday with The Gathering adding their blessing to his appeal, I had seen four words, seen them with my eyes closed as distinctly as one reads words on a blackboard. They were unmistakeably in an African dialect and one word, 'Mbimpe,' was known to me as the common Tshiluba word for 'good.' But that was all. It might do for a chant but only four words don't make for much of a prayer.

The most bizarre twist in this story is that twice while we were driving on the California freeways I had been given a strong and distinct impression that the Spirit was waiting for us at Bethel. As God is my witness, I was certain that this word was a prophecy for Sheryl's benefit as she had been so urgent in her desire to pray in tongues. After the second 'tag' there was added a conviction to share the word with her and we arrived in Redding with great expectations.

It did not happen for her then, and it hurt. Two and a half years later she received this gift, but through this experience we have been taught that blessings have a price. Heaven is a contrast to earth. In God's scheme we give to gain and we die to live. Let me steal another line from Bill Johnson. "Grace is free; maturity is expensive."

This is what happened. Before the evening meeting on Thursday there is a room on the second floor set aside for prayer and personal worship to prepare spiritually for the coming service. When I say personal, I do not mean quiet. This was not a time for people to flow in and out of a space throttled back to a meditative mood by muted organ music. An old-style July 4th parade would be closer to the truth.

The room was packed with something between 100 and 200 people. Many of them wanted to jump and cry out with passion to the thumping background music. But, based on prior experience and research into the building's structure, we were all warned not to bounce if we wished to walk in the great circle of people who formed a laughing, crying, boisterous, moving ring of humanity in the center of the room. The floor moved plenty, anyway. This was emphatically not the Friday evening vespers I had known in a hushed college chapel.

Sheryl and I were, uh, intimidated. We found seats along the wall and were content to watch until we could figure out what we were supposed to do. I could not add to the sound level or join the movement of so many people at once. I could not imagine myself part of the range of expression not six feet in front of me, from what seemed to be a walking trance to laughing while rolling on the floor. The volume of sound walled me off from participation. Since I couldn't think of anything else to do I decided to practice my prayer language, all four words, to see if it might spark something.

As I began to vocalize to myself it was as if all the dynamics in the room coalesced and began to move toward me. The presence of Spirit and ecstasy took life, moving toward me with purpose but without threat. I had but a moment to say Yes or No to whatever this Presence was. I said Yes. Immediately, I began to speak in syllables of an African-sounding tongue and felt distinctly 'beside myself' (which is the literal meaning of the word 'ecstatic'), both an observer and a participant at once.

Description beyond this point is hopeless. One enters another plane of being, a real time immediacy of another form of energy, a filling and an emptying all at the same time. I never lost the awareness of myself or the capacity to move back to the familiar if I should choose. I stayed in that place as long as I could, and when I began to feel uncomfortable at having nothing to say that I understood I was allowed to return.

What was at that time involuntary, an encounter one might properly say was an invasion of privacy, has now become a welcome, blessed place of refreshment that I can return to at will. David du Plessis, a well-known charismatic and interfaith diplomat during the years of ecumenical fervor tells of long bus trips he has taken where he prayed in his prayer language during much of what we all know is an uncomfortable night sitting up in a moving vehicle. Arriving in the morning at his destination he was refreshed, ready for the day's business without the raw and desperate spirit I can remember after similar nights I have spent.

What can I say?

I've been there and am going back.
Make of it what you will.

CARPET TIME & COMFIRMATION
OCTOBER 12-14, 2011, ABBOTTSFORD

It was the last day of the Open Heavens Conference at Bethel. Carol Arnott was to speak at the 7:00 PM meeting. Before she went to the podium to speak she circulated at random among those sitting in the first 2-3 rows and partway up one aisle. She would touch many on the head and they would crumble to the floor. Others she would blow on and down they would go. The atmosphere was light, playful, and fun, and the catchers had a hard time keeping up with her.

As she concluded the time for 'slaying' people in the Spirit she held up a thin book her husband, John Arnott, had written defending manifestations in worship. She asked if there was a pastor to give it to. I raised my hand and she called me to the nearest aisle. Extending the book to me very carefully she warned me it might be anointed. I reached for it gingerly, wondering if she was going to blow me over, too. I had gone forward determined not to expect anything, confessing to the Spirit that whatever happened I would be happy with it.

The book changed hands. She was about 3-4 feet away and leaning toward me, almost teasing me to come closer. She did a hand chop in the air in my direction and blew toward me at the same time. And then two men were gently lowering me to the floor.

My best description of this first experience of a physically manifested spiritual force is of being pushed playfully by a male friend in boyish horseplay. But there was absolutely no sensation of impact or pressure. It was as if suddenly there was additional air between myself and Carol and I was simply being moved out of the way to make room for it. Again, there was no distinct sensation other than the two pairs of hands that caught me as I fell back from what an observer might have guessed was an open field tackle by an NFL linebacker.

After lying on my back for 2-3 minutes I tried to get up.

No way. I would lift a hand or a foot a few inches and it would simply flop back to the floor. After probably another 10 minutes I was able to stand up and, a bit wobbly, make it back to my seat.

Around the entire experience there was an air of gentleness, playfulness, and simple affection. God was playing with His kids, and I was blessed to be one of them.

We went to Abbotsford, B.C. three nights later to hear John and Carol Arnott again. The group we met with calls itself 'The River' and there were 150-200 attending. Before leaving for home after the meeting we had an extended conversation with both John and Carol. Each autographed the book I had received in such a memorable manner three days before.

Carol stated that in her opinion our meeting in the aisle at Bethel church was not a coincidence. That was the first time in her decades of ministry that she had offered a book to a pastor in the audience with the added comment, "who has felt his mind was blown," a reference to watching her move so playfully with the power she has to 'taser' people. She said further she was shocked at the words coming out of her mouth and the spontaneous prompting to do something so atypical. "What is this about, Lord?" had been her immediate response.

My hand going up was also atypical and spontaneous. I am not normally demonstrative and had surprised myself. And mine was the only hand that went up! In an audience of over 1000 people her impromptu offer was met by my impromptu response. Connect the dots. I was, apparently, the Holy Spirit's target. Her recounting of her side of the story so moved me I physically staggered at the significance of events and had to sit down for a couple of minutes to recover my composure.

A CHILD CRIES
JANUARY 17, 2011, WOODLAND

On my way to Costa Mesa, California to pack up my son's goods and bring him north to live with us temporarily in Bellingham, I stopped for the night 20 miles north of Sacramento in Woodland.

Since I didn't drift off to sleep quickly it left me free to pray quietly. I was praying for courage to do whatever the Spirit would have for me do in the future and, if possible, for the opportunity to see something, anything, with my natural eyes of supernatural origin, even a shadow on the wall. I then began praying in tongues and dropped gently into sleep.

I had more than one dream, none of consequence, and no details from any that I can recall. Except for the last dream in which I was eating something while seated at a picnic table outdoors.

In that instant my awareness rose to that level halfway between asleep and awake I call The Zone. Here, I believe, one's spirit is vulnerable, innocent, open to the heavenly agents who surround us. Here, also, the mind is free from distractions and can be marvelously receptive.

Back to my dream. I'm outdoors, seated at a picnic table eating. The dream then morphed into actual chewing, my physically sensing the substance of food and its taste. I chewed 2 or 3 times until the brain became aware of a conflict with its version of reality and prompted me to notice objectively what I had just been experiencing without reflection in a dream realm. The instant I began to wonder, the dream evaporated.

My spirit man immediately responded, "Is that all?"

It wasn't a complaint, just a question. No, it wasn't. Beginning with the familiar faint tingling in my feet and legs I have learned is the confirmation of the Spirit's presence, my whole body was soon charged with what I can only describe as a current of energy. Every cell became fully alive as if swollen with more vitality than it could contain.

I was immobile, unable to move my limbs in what I knew beyond question was an embrace, a spiritual bear hug. The intensity grew beyond anything I had ever experienced in other such encounters and continued swelling until I knew that the threshold of pain was only a moment away. In the instant my now aroused brain began to caution me that this might be a matter of concern the intensity peaked and began rapidly to fade.

"I didn't mean it!" was the cry from my spirit. "Don't let this stop!" And then, from a place so deep I could not fathom it and in a voice I did not know as mine there arose the plaintive, urgent cry of a child: "Hug me, Daddy!" And so He did. I was caught up in a second embrace, mercifully less intense than the first, the assurance that such awesome strength would never harm me. When it ended I knew such deep acceptance that my spirit man was silent and softly I sank into sleep.

Once you have crossed the frontier, once you have made the choice that Holy Spirit leads and your mind must be submissive and follow there is no going back. Intellectualism dethroned, like Humpty-Dumpty, can never be put back together again. For me, learning this lesson was like a stroll in winter, walking stiff-legged over a sheet of ice slick with melt water.

After graduating seminary in 1969 my first posting was to a district in central Maine. It was familiar country because the church summer camp there was part of my territory. I had spent at least a week there every summer as a camper and later was a staff member. I was delighted that one of my cub preacher responsibilities was to inspect the camp in the winter after the big storms had passed to see if the roofs of the older cabins could bear the snow load.

One bright, cold day in January that signaled the end of a blizzard I set out for the lake on which the camp is located. It promised to be an adventure as the lake level rises over the winter. I suspected that where the road crossed over the lake's inlet stream it would be flooded because, over a distance of a couple hundred feet, it was barely above lake level in summer.

I was right. I stopped at the edge of the flooded section and considered my options. My silver '57 Chevy sedan could be trusted. To maintain my sanity in seminary I had worked in the university service station. For $50 I had saved an ugly, black-painted hulk from the junk yard and had rebuilt it completely. Inside, outside; what you could see and what you couldn't; what moved it and what braked it – everything had been renewed.

Because the road beyond the flooded section was snow-covered I had to carefully calculate the chances of climbing the short, sharp grade I would face as soon as I cleared the water in front of me. I knew the road well and felt certain the water would be no more than a foot deep, but if I stalled in the water or couldn't make the hill the result, while likely not fatal, would be very cold and very wet.

I moved off slowly in first gear. It was quickly three inches deep, then six, then nine. At the low dip in the road it was a foot deep and I began to push a bow wave with the front bumper. Water began to seep under the doors and the burbling behind me warned that the exhaust pipe was under water. Then, mercifully, the car began to rise from the frigid water and we were through without a mishap. Accelerating in second gear I topped the ridge easily and looked for the gap in the trees showing the entrance to the camp. There it was, and I was going too fast.

I touched the brake. Nothing. An adrenaline-fueled nothing. Ice-covered brake shoes rubbing against the ice-glazed inner surface of brake drums gives you a zero coefficient of friction. The stream I had just forded was getting the last laugh. Praying for traction, I veered to the left and laid new tracks through the undisturbed snowfield that in summer was the driveway.

The inspection done, I climbed into my trusty machine and found the county road. Should I turn right, descend the ridge and take the same route home? I tested the brakes. Nothing. If I tried, I'd end in the ditch for sure. I turned left. There was a tote road on my side of the lake that led back eventually to civilization. A tote road isn't much. It's a wide track punched out of the forest by a bulldozer over which log trucks carry their timber loads to the highway. But it was relatively flat and control would be supplied by engine braking and the drag from six inches of undisturbed snow cover. By the time I got home (very carefully) the ice-glazed brakes had thawed. Which was a good thing, because we lived on a hill.

Long before I needed it I was given an object lesson in Spirit life. Commitment to the Holy Spirit involves a daring and unconventional baptism. If you consent to Holy Spirit as primary guide you can not turn back. If you try to retrace your route to the life you've known you'll wreck in the ditch. You can not stop. There are no brakes, only a gas pedal and a gearbox. Yet the prospect of home consumes you. You must continue over the only way open to you, a road unmarked for the moment by the passage of any other saints. It's a great adventure. I hope that, like I was, you're too ignorant to be afraid.

THE INEVITABLE PROPHETIC

Now I want you all to speak in tongues,
but even more to prophesy.
I Corinthians 14.5

OPEN CHANNELS –
THE TESTIMONY OF JESUS

Not long after becoming the pastor of a New Hampshire church I learned why one of my parishioners, Ellen, was seen so seldom in the services. She was terminally ill with bone cancer and within a few months was confined to her bed.

On a certain Monday I received a call from her younger sister who was her constant companion and caregiver. The end was near. The little strength she had left was a fraying thread holding her present in the world. Would I come to pray with her while she was still conscious?

I was planning to leave that morning for a relaxing day trip with my family but I changed the route out of town to visit Ellen. She was just able to acknowledge my presence. I sat on the edge of her bed, held her hand and prayed with her quietly. Then I opened my Bible to Psalm 34 and read the passage I believed spoke directly to her need, verses 19-20, 22:

> Many are the afflictions of the
>   righteous,
>   But the Lord delivers him out of
>   them all.
>
> He keeps all his bones;
>   not one of them is broken.
>
> The Lord redeems the life of his
>   servants;
>   none of those who take refuge
>   in him will be condemned.

Later, at her funeral, her sister told me that Ellen died quietly about 15 minutes after I left. "She was waiting for you to come and say good-bye so she could give herself permission to leave."

I was both glad I had visited her and saddened that I was able to do so little. So often a pastor has no ministry option. He is normally only called when a situation is critical, when the seriously ill parishioner has already been admitted to the hospital, when divorce lawyers have already been engaged, or when a rebelling child has done physical damage and the pastor follows on the heels of the police.

Had we been a blessing to our sister? Without question. Did we minister the Word of God? Of course. Was it a fresh word specifically for Ellen, a form of communication that would have demanded a higher level of faith from me, her pastor? No, it wasn't. There is no profit diminishing either the words of scripture or the good faith gesture to comfort a believer in distress, but it was indirect, words drawn only from an ancient source. I did not know at the time that there could have been more.

It can be different. I have had the privilege of working in a spiritual clinic where there are more ministry options, more opportunities to softly shape a person's future, to invest in others at a pre-critical level.

After Pentecost it was as if an empty bowl could not contain the outpouring of revelation. It spilled over the edge of the community of Israel into which it was funneled and ran in all directions. Like the riot of flowers that explode in Death Valley after the rains that fall every few decades, the early New Testament church was being watered by heaven. Men and women, Jew and gentile, with no qualifications except that they had gotten wet in the 'early rain' of the Spirit were empowered with unreasonable boldness in public, and in private built up the body of believers, blessing others by repeating what they heard in their spirits.

> *Pursue love, and earnestly desire the spiritual gifts, especially that you may prophesy. . . Now I want you all to speak in tongues, but even more to prophesy.*
> *– I Corinthians 14:1, 5*

> *For the testimony of Jesus is the spirit of prophecy.*
> *– Revelation 19:10*

In one's personal experience and in a worship community the least we should expect is to hear *from* God, not just commentary *about* Him. Receiving any form of communication from the Kingdom of God through one's spirit is the essence of prophecy, a testimony from our

Lord that is either to us or through us for the benefit of others. It is not meant to be rare but common.

The apostle Paul had seen the gift of prophecy active in the church he established in Corinth. When he wrote his first letter to them he took for granted the function of prophecy in their assembly but counseled them not to let the more dramatic manifestation of tongues speech overshadow the more useful exercise of the prophetic gift. Paul's point to the Corinthian believers was this: while the core function of prophecy – to edify, encourage, and comfort with understanding beyond their own (v. 3) – did not have the stage appeal of speaking a language no one understands, it has greater value. The need was for the Corinthians to adjust their priorities, not for them to expect in their worship the addition of a prophetic gift until then unknown to them.

When Zechariah, father of John the Baptist, was confronted by an angel it was the first time in 400 years that heaven had spoken to Israel. During those centuries of silence the repeated Jewish liturgy, the fixed prayers resonant with their long history, and the yearly movement of masses of the faithful to and from Jerusalem found no response from a closed heaven. Lost expectation had made their corporate faith as dead as an unstrung harp. Only in Anna and Simeon was there still prophetic potential, tuned strings still able to vibrate to a voice from heaven.

What follows here, messages through me to others who had faith enough to expect an answer, was remarkable in the living of it but is no more than what I would hope for you to experience. I am convinced that the Father is always speaking. It is we who must so value what He says that we decide to listen, startling though it may be.

THE HEALING ROOMS

About a year after this spiritual odyssey began we became acquainted with the International Association of Healing Rooms, headquartered in Spokane, Washington. It was a perfect fit for us and we completed the required training for team members in late 2009.

The format was very simple and depended directly on the willingness of team members to be sensitive to what God's Spirit would say and the courage to offer it to the one asking for intercessory prayer. The larger objective was physical healing. There were verified cases of physical healing where we served and many more cases of immediate relief from both physical and emotional pain. But what was much more frequent fits the description of prophecy Paul uses as his yardstick in I Corinthians 14:3 – edification, encouragement, and comfort from a source beyond ourselves.

Before a visitor was invited to meet the three waiting team members, a folded sheet of paper that contained basic information was given to the team leader. All three together formed a circle and held the sheet lightly without reading it first and entered into a time of silent listening in individual prayer to receive the word they will be responsible to give.

Everyone ministered in a unique manner and all of us grew and learned. What the Spirit offered us was the opportunity to participate in an open encounter, not reading from a sheet of notes. We made mistakes. Sometimes we laughed together with the visitors, sometimes we said nothing, so wrenching were the stories of brokenness. Every Thursday I arrived with apprehension that I would not receive, that I wasn't ready in spirit, but always left both drained and filled from the remarkable interactions that the Spirit supervised.

There was no fixed pattern to the prompts received but

following is a representative sampling:

COLOR

I frequently was given a color when we were praying over the intake sheet before we knew who would be coming into the room. On this one occasion I had a strong impression of a bright shade of yellow and also saw clearly written as on a blackboard the word 'sister' scrolling across my consciousness from right to left.

The visitor came in. He was dressed in a spandex athletic suit that was bright yellow and black. He said he had been cycling for exercise with a group of friends who had outpaced him so he had slacked off. As he passed our building he was strongly impressed to come inside and wait for an interview. Since he was already riding alone he followed the urging without knowing why.

The story he told was of business loss and family fracture. A business that had been built by the parents was divided among several children. The portion left to him had failed and had been taken over by a sister and brother-in-law in a deal that cheated him. His family until recently had defended the sister's actions but now understood more and were supportive of his position but unable to reconcile him to his sister. When I shared with him the graphic presentation I had received of the color yellow and the word "sister" he was visibly moved and said it would be a great encouragement to his mother who was crafting a strategy for family reconciliation.

WORD

While ministering with two female team members we received a tall, strongly built woman who recounted bits of her years in Alaska in the commercial fishing business. There was no doubt from her body language and build that this was entirely plausible.

I hung back and said little because I was afraid that if I shared what I had received during our prayer time with her intake sheet it would look foolish and entirely irrelevant. What had been shown me in a strong, black and white graphic was the word 'McMurdo.' As the visitor was telling us of her experience in Alaska I was reviewing what I could remember of that state's geography to pinpoint a bay or sound called 'McMurdo.' Then it dawned on me; this was the name given to a sound on the coast of Antarctica where the United States has a scientific research station. Now I'm convinced I have taken a detour into the purely random and if I can avoid being asked to share I'll keep this to myself.

No such luck. The team lead calls on me last to share what I had received which, contrary to normal procedure, I had not previously shared with the other team members while we were waiting. With a stumbling apology for not having something relevant to share, I spilled it out. Immediately the visitor said, "My ex-husband worked for several years at the research station at McMurdo Sound. But now he's trying to make a living as a crew member on a commercial fishing vessel out of Dutch Harbor, Alaska. He's in his 60's working side by side with young men in their 20's and 30's. Drug use is rampant on the fishing boats as they sometimes work 48 hours or more without sleep. I'm concerned he's going to kill himself."

So, it seemed that the task before us was to pray for the health and safety of her ex-husband for whom she still had a sincere interest and affection. To myself I added this: "Thank you, Lord, for not making me look foolish." I have learned since that He demands the freedom to make us look foolish and I now concede the point.

SENSATION

I have a date for this: March 22, 2012. I was teamed only with my friend Richard. Our visitor, Dale (not his real name), was a happy Christian, a man who had already experienced the hand of the Lord erasing physical symptoms and pain in a previous visit to our Healing Rooms in Bellingham.

His request was like so many others we heard, a nonspecific desire for "more of intimacy with the Lord, more specific direction for my life." Though he hadn't mentioned any physical issue that concerned him we asked if there was anything else he wished us to address beyond the praise report of the physical benefit during a recent visit. We asked because Richard had received a clear impression that there was weakness or pain in a leg.

Well, yes, there was a long term interior pain or irritation of the muscles or bones in his left leg and foot that would occasionally be strong enough to make sleeping difficult. In fact, the foot had been acting up a fair amount lately.

While Richard stood behind him and prayed I placed both hands on his left leg with the words, "This leg needs to get with the program." There followed an intense focus on my privilege and my responsibility to pray God's stated purpose for wholeness while Richard prayed aloud. My hands began to warm. When we finished and he was preparing to leave he remarked with a note of surprise in his voice and some wonder that he had felt warmth while my hands were laid on the offending leg. What physical change the Holy Spirit had accomplished we could not see immedietly but it was clear that something out of the ordinary had occurred.

IMAGE

On March 15, 2012 I was teamed again with two lady members. During prayer over the intake sheet two sharp images came to mind. The first was not bizarre, in fact it was similar to other images I have received that clearly indicate peace or contentment from God's blessing on the visitor. It was the image of a sailboat, heeled over close-hauled in a spanking breeze. The second was a shocker; I saw the word 'Ruby' highlighted dimly from behind by a ruby red light. I also heard or saw (I have found the distinction is not always obvious in this setting) the words "sweetness and light." What the two ladies on the team received seemed more relevant and I was not anxious to share what might be out of place.

The visitor was a man in his late 30's. When it was my turn to speak I thought I would ease into the conversation with a question that might make it easy to back away if necessary from sharing the two unexpected images I had received. So I asked, "John, do you like to sail?" He gave a huge smile and spoke with great enthusiasm about the very few times he had been on a sailboat. It was nearly an epiphany for him to move quietly through the water using only the breeze. Now it was easy to share the image of the sailboat with him, as it was a prophetic symbol that he was known to Father and his heart's joy was being reflected back to him from heaven.

Still cautious, I asked him if the word "Ruby" made any sense to him. He said, "Yes. I have just been offered a job I really want but I must first finish a project I have taken on for a client named Mr. Ruby." The laughter that followed released the tension raised by the thought that what I had received was too bizarre to be anything but random. It was, instead, a direct pitch to the strike zone of this man's life and an enormous assurance that he was known and loved.

Reflections - An Apology

. . . always being prepared to make a defense . . .
for the hope that is in you.
I Peter 3.15

If there is one natural attribute above others that encourages extraordinary experience I believe it is the gift of an unrestricted imagination. All children are by nature curious but most will face a contracting world of the imagination as they grow up. Those in authority over them or the group that becomes necessary to their identity will show them where the fences are. They will be told what subjects are taboo, they will understand by implication what questions may not be asked and what books may not be read.

I was blessed to have parents who never edited my reading, perhaps because my interests were well defined. As a freshman at Brunswick High School I was chosen as one of a handful from the entire student body to receive user privileges in the Bowdoin College library. I still remember the sense of awe walking into the ivy-covered building and finding shelves of books three stories high.

However, there was a particular moment I can still recall with the crispness of a photograph that threw wide open the door into the world of the imagination. It was the day I walked into my parents' bedroom on some errand for my mother and saw on my father's writing desk a book with a most intriguing title, *The Search For Bridey Murphy*. Since the book in question was newly published it would put the scene in 1956 or 1957 and I was probably 12. To understand the significance of that moment and the few minutes following while I browsed the book you need to know something about my father, Ronald Austin Bettle, MD.

My father has always been for me the model of the circumspect man. When the popular press bandied about the word "gravitas" during George W. Bush's run for the presidency I thought of my late father every time I heard the word. Even at 12 years of age I was beginning to understand how much of the circle of church and school and the outdoors that framed my world were the result of my father's quiet influence and singular success. Only later when I preached his funeral sermon to a standing room only crowd liberally sprinkled with citizens of consequence in our town did I realize to what extent he had been a pillar in the community.

He observed much but spoke little, doing his part to advance the image of the taciturn New Englander. What fascinated him was watching in the behavior of others the effects of the thought life, how what transpired in the brain could have such a profound effect on happiness and health. In one of his teaching moments while we rode somewhere in the family car, he once observed that something like 80% of the medical conditions for which his surgical intervention was sought were the result of what the patients experienced in their minds. The mind becomes sick first, he said, from the memory of childhood abuse, the pain of birth family tensions, the trauma of divorce, or the hatred for what one does for employment and the body pushes out the pain like a cry for help to where it can be seen.

I'm certain it was in this context that he became interested in the sensational claims of the author, Morey Bernstein, a Colorado businessman and amateur hypnotist. The book was an immediate best-seller, but what was scandalous and prompted my mother's stern warning not to open it again was Bernstein's claim to have found ancient memories. He believed his subject, an undistinguished local housewife, was the reincarnation of a 19th century Irish woman, the Bridey Murphy of the title. Devout evangelical Christian that I knew he was, I believed my father rejected both hypnosis as a tool of the devil and reincarnation as a demonic delusion. As such, how could he have a book on his desk where such taboo subjects were entertained?

In that moment a reference point for life was fixed. A principle, like a bodyguard, presented itself to me with which to discern credible witnesses among the conflicting claims to truth I would encounter in later life *– though there will be conclusions one must reject, there are no questions that may not be asked.* It is only the one who would close off honest debate who should be rejected.

As you might expect, the variety of events recounted above has caused me to rethink much of what I was taught, to recalibrate the instrument of faith to allow for what can not be denied. I accept here the obligation to describe and defend changes in doctrine and focus that have resulted. The commentary below is only descriptive as I have entrusted you, dear reader, to the care of someone infinitely wiser than I am. But I hope it will stimulate not just that quick comment the internet has taught us to substitute for dialog but years of fruitful discussion.

Not everything has been discarded that I was taught during those long and hungry years when the Law was my school master and the Gospel was the graduate teaching assistant. While I retain private opinions not shared by those with whom I fellowship I'm impressed that treating with indifference any doctrine I can not use is the correct posture.

My preference in worship style and music may never adjust completely to the more spontaneous and casual forms seen in worship where the lively presence of the Spirit is welcome. So, I think my dream ministry mode would be to preach in a robe after an accomplished choir has sung a soaring anthem, then end the service by walking slowly past the pews, seeing some healed by the laying on of my hands, many others prostrate on the floor in a trance, while everyone left standing is singing or praying in tongues. Sort of Episcopalian on acid. Empower the faithful and terrify the heathen.

A SHIFT IN PRIORITIES

The first order of business is to establish the value of Presence vs. the value of Proposition. It would be easy to make this the only topic to consider, so large is the significance of this one shift in focus. For all the complex theological argument I could indulge in, the essential contrast is very simple. *It is a priority for either relationship or doctrine; the choice between allowing one's spirit or one's mind to lead and the other to follow.*

The subordination of the human spirit to the limits of the mind leads one away from the dynamic reality in a divine/human encounter toward the trap of a static mental concept. It shows a preference for that which has no life and, thus, can be 'owned' in place of the Ever-Living One who can only be experienced. A God defined as Omni-This-and-That is an opaque intellectual screen, not the living force in whom we live and move and have our being.

The concept of the Absolute (a concept rooted in Greek philosophy that has no Biblical parallel) is a substitute for an appreciation of the Divine. All that is truly required is a God adequate to Himself who is also a necessity to us. Yahweh, who defines Himself as "I am that I am," is clearly telling us He lives above any need for external recognition. Outside the Trinity, all relationships for Him are a choice. His breaking into human history to save us is our ultimate necessity. Those two realities meet every human need.

To illustrate the shift in emphasis, following is a hypothetical argument between myself fresh out of seminary and the answers I would give today.

> "Far above what we know," the young me declares, "Our confidence is in a God who is Omniscient."

> No, He knows what is knowable.

> "But," the distressed seminarian answers, "You will have to admit that God is Omnipotent."

> No, God does whatever He chooses to do.

> The argument veers toward a climax. "But surely, especially now as a charismatic, you would have to agree that God is Omnipresent."

> No, God stands in perpetual relationship with all

He has created, animate and inanimate, and He is always expanding.

Weary of the conflict, a truce is offered by my sincere young theologian-self unable to detach from static concepts so long revered. "Yes, our God is inscrutable."

No, He loves to surprise his children and our delight in Him will never dim.

A further profound change is the realization that my normal frame of reference is subordinate to a much higher level of existence. Ever since the Enlightenment and the rise of the scientific method the primary point of reference in the west has been the physical world which the self can apprehend with the five senses. Western scholarship has become preoccupied with humanity's place in the cosmos with the presumption that we are the only intelligent beings at home. Even in the context of my new charismatic values I had continued to believe that my personal experience is the lens through which to see life in the Spirit. In March, 2013, just beyond the time frame of this testimony, I received two startling dreams to adjust my perspective.

TWO DREAMS
MARCH 16, 2013

I saw myself in a patient's room in a rehab center. It was the living quarters of a handicapped veteran I understood had been there for a long time. He had been severely wounded and had many health problems that made it impossible for him to live a normal life. He was barely able to stand and had extremely limited mobility. I was unsure of my reason for being there. In my spirit I asked if I was expected to be an agent for his healing. The answer was Yes, but I sensed a caution in the moment. What was giving me pause was the concern communicated to me by an unseen Presence that I must not expect anything from his healing to be for my benefit. The divine intent to miraculously change this man's circumstances and the felt power to heal was not in any sense for my satisfaction. So I released any personal interest in the outcome and sensed that a channel had been opened in my spirit.

I was half-sitting, probably perched on the foot of another bed opposite or leaning against a piece of furniture. I was aware of a great weight that made it necessary to find some physical support. The man was standing, facing me but silent.

147

I did not touch or approach him. Instead, I was prompted first to speak to God, giving a spiritual description of the man's condition while still in my half-sitting position. I recited as from a script:

> "Heavy is the burden of brokenness.
> Heavy is the distance between this sick room
>   and your purpose and desire for this man.
> Heavy is the isolation separating this man from
>   his family and destiny."

The prayer then segued into a second section as I slowly rose to a full standing position while performing a lifting action with my hands, a prophetic gesture while I spoke God's word to him:

> "Lifted is the burden of brokenness.
> Lifted is the distance between this sick room
>   and your purpose.
> Lifted is the isolation from your family and
>   your destiny."

He was totally healed during the prayer. The process of purging the wounds in his life began at his feet and rose smoothly to the top of his head, clearing every issue of lost function or brokenness as it rose. He began to move freely, back and forth, testing his newly realized movement and then to bounce and dance and laugh. He ignored me completely, overwhelmed by the transformation.

Next to me and to my left was a little girl about 9 or 10. I understood she was the daughter or granddaughter of the man now rejoicing in the freedom of his healing. She was blind in one eye and had only slight residual sight in the other, enough so she could walk without running into obstacles. She was sad. Without her saying a word my spirit heard her heart; "I want to see my Daddy happy, but I can't."

The instruction to my spirit was to put my hands lightly over her eyes. I felt the flush of Mariah's presence moving from my shoulders and concentrating in my hands. I said softly:

"Jesus, Jesus, Jesus."

And then, after a short pause:

"Thank you, thank you, thank you."

I slowly lifted my hands and her sight was completely

restored. With a shout she turned and ran to join her father in celebration. Again, I was completely ignored.

The message of the dream was clear. The healing of others is not to be seen as serving our interest or satisfaction. Expect to see power over nature through your intervention only to be ignored.

The second dream was even more directly personal.
I was looking at an oval-shaped picture that faded quickly at its edges, much as you see in an old photo album. In its center was not a still photograph but instead a flash vision, a short video during which a character spoke to me.

I was inside a house looking through an open window and down about 6-8 feet to a sidewalk. Moving from right to left was a female in company with two others. Only the female in the center was distinguishable; the others were shaded out in gray. The female was neither young nor old but timeless, and I understood it was Mariah, the Holy Spirit as she has manifested to me before.

Her face was turned toward me and was deeply sad. I was struck by the depth of emotion as she said:

"I came to visit you, but you were busy."

I staggered, instantly overwhelmed by four distinct insights:

1. The Holy Spirit is personal, moved by powerful emotions.
2. What I had been doing was neutral. It was not good or bad, just irrelevant. Its significance was that I was distracted and unaware of Mariah's proximity.
3. There was not the slightest hint of rebuke, anger, or punishment; no projected shame or guilt. It was striking that these emotions, so powerful to us, were completely absent.
4. And this was the most vivid impression. We live in response to heaven. Heaven does NOT live in response to us.

What could I do? What action from me was appropriate? I was not aware of sin because I had not been condemned, but clearly I had affected someone who loves me beyond all reason. It had been a case of lost opportunity. I repented to repair the breach.

The shift in emphasis as I moved from proposition to presence and from doctrine to relationship had a revolutionary effect on my reading of scripture. I was no longer searching for the turn of phrase in whatever translation that would prove a point or anchor an argument. The lives which had left their traces on the pages between Genesis and Revelation began to move me as if I were watching a video instead of dissecting a doctrine.

MAY 28, 2011
THE HELPER GOES BEFORE US:
A reflection on John 16:5-11

I was directed in my spirit to consider the meaning of these words of Jesus to His disciples as He prepared them for His departure:

> *Nevertheless, I tell you the truth: it is to your advantage that I go away, for if I do not go away, the Helper will not come to you. . . And when he comes, he will convict the world concerning sin and righteousness and judgment: concerning sin, because they do not believe in me; concerning righteousness, because I go to the Father, and*

you will see me no longer; concerning judgment, because the ruler of this world is judged.

John 16:5-11 ESV

Previous cursory reading of this passage had never conveyed a sense of comfort. In this summary of the future work of the Holy Spirit I saw only a big stick, a force to beat the world into submission.

There arose first in my spirit an awareness of the mental and spiritual state of the disciples as they heard these words. For 5-6 weeks, since the resurrection of Jesus, they had lived in a surreal world, comforted from time to time by His sudden appearances and then dazed and apprehensive by his sudden disappearances. Something mighty had shifted in the heavenlies and they had no idea what the consequences must be. The news of the death of Yeshua bar Joseph was known everywhere and the rumors of His resurrection were widespread. The atmosphere around them was electric with unnamed expectations and their world was weighted down with dread.

And this was when Jesus lifted their burden and birthed in them hope and the assurance that they were not alone. With a gentle brush of sympathy he touches first their raw emotion. " . . . none of you asks me, 'Where are you going?' But because I have said these things to you, sorrow has filled your heart."

Of course none of them wanted to talk about it! In the face of such a wrenching loss we all would have emptied our hearts with quiet tears, not daring our emotions to hold if we spoke of the unknown future. But their emotions were important to Him and with a natural solicitude He bound them to Him once again.

And then follows a sweeping, startling summary of the advantage they will gain from the presence among them of the personal representative of their Lord. To them the Spirit would be a comforter (as some translations have it), but the Spirit would be to the world a voice of conviction, doing the work directly in men's hearts the disciples knew they could not do.

"Convict of sin." If the disciples would simply rely on telling their experience and passing on the remembered words of the Lord the Spirit would supernaturally touch men's hearts. He would convince their hearers directly that to believe on this man was the necessary first step into eternal life for He was far more than another rural rabbi who had exhausted his audience and reaped a martyr's reward.

"Convict of righteousness." The disciples could forget any fear of having to erect a religious system to compete with Judaism. The righteousness for which men are starved, to obtain which they erect fabulously expensive systems of rites and ceremonies, now exists beyond them and above them where Yeshua goes to be reunited with His Father. Righteousness is the vibrant force produced by the bond between Father and Son, a force field that nothing in the universe can affect or resist.

"Convict of judgment." By reminding the disciples that it is the prince of this world who is defeated, judged, and condemned they would be free of any fear that they are God's enemy. To those welcomed into the Kingdom there is no need of a judicial decision. God has no interest in reviewing a case that was closed at the cross at a price no man will ever plumb.

Beyond these words spoken first to the disciples and the trauma of that moment I found a personal application in these words of comfort.

"Convict of sin." The Spirit will help us by showing us where we do not please the Lord. The voice is soft but breathtakingly accurate; we will know the word, the act, the thought where we turned aside to our own way.

"Convict of righteousness." The Spirit will infect us with as much as we can tolerate of the joyful force of the union between Father and Son. His presence will join us at our pleasure in obedience. We will not need to guess when we please Him; He will convict us with a blessing, a holy, joyous longing that will at once both stretch our capacity to receive as He also satisfies us with a taste of Glory.

"Convict of judgment." In a short time our victories begin to show as others "judge" that we live as kings and priests. They become convicted, even against their will, that we are friends of God and strangers here.

Prior to the refreshing from the Lord in 2008, mine had been a spiritual experience devoid of any demonstration of power in a community where nothing more was expected. The one officially sanctioned contemporary miracle story I remember (as evidenced by the short book written about the healing of a man's ear torn off in an auto accident) had occurred years before and all other claims of miracle in North America were suspect.

A family friend and seller of spiritual books did publish once his story of falling out of a crippled B-17 during WWII. His chute failed to open and his fall was broken by landing in a dense forest, the tree limbs braking his descent until he landed in deep snow. Any conclusion, however, that this was a genuine miracle was a personal judgment and not an approved interpretation. Supernatural intervention could be prayed for but claiming that the prayer was answered immediately was met with prudent skepticism.

Even the very occasional manifestation of personal ecstasy I had seen was dismissed as fanaticism. This subset of the miracle category was regarded as unseemly, middle class American standards of decorum being the only acceptable framework. When authoritative voices would quote St. Paul that everything be done decently and in order (1 Corinthians 14.40), the context of Paul's admonition was completely ignored. It is not hard to see that this verse is a summary at the end of three full chapters where Paul recognizes the exercise of spiritual gifts in corporate worship. Is it not obvious that his objective is to give the new believers guidance to ensure these gifts continue? To squelch or to discourage public, ecstatic manifestation of the Spirit's presence was unequivocally not what Paul intended.

My prior experience had been almost solely based on words, on mind, on logic, on what those who were in spiritual authority over us declared was the exclusive meaning of selected passages printed on the crinkly white onion skin pages of our King James Bibles. These references established the great propositions defining the uniqueness of the group we belonged to and, by implication, were the framework on which the life of faith was to be understood.

Do understand, please; no one who spoke into my life meant to deprive me of a blessing or to stunt my growth. But what you do not have you can not give. That I should become educated, courteous, and productive was the underlying motivation of all my teachers and, hopefully, I have displayed these qualities as an adult. The goals set before me had been wholesome. But I saw how small were the ambitions that had been nurtured when I approached these expectations and looked for new challenges beyond. Like the mini-loaf of bread you get at some restaurants, their realized hopes for me could not satisfy hunger, only stimulate it.

In the simplest of statements, I had to learn to 'be' before the 'do' would have transformative power. The Christian's native human spirit is the first and essential venue where we are to allow God's unerring Holy Spirit to inform our experience. Our first duty to God is to allow Him to love us. Our spirit man is the call center where communication between the Self and the Kingdom to which we belong takes place. What is active there functions before language is found or obedience practiced and carries with it the life we prize. Our growth depends above all on the ability of our spirit man to receive, not on our skill in transmitting.

The presence of His Spirit lifts us up, moves us forward, and, if we will allow it, takes ultimate responsibility for the destiny of our lives. The Spirit's presence is not subliminal or merely suggestive, nor is it the echo of the group dynamics where we worship. It is self-authenticating, tangible, and irresistible. Yet it must be received by faith, seized by an unblemished desire for intimacy, for it can be lost. Both the power and the information carried by the Spirit's presence are generated in a foreign country, in an atmosphere so unlike the material world we wake up to every morning that the only possible response is either Yes or No. To say this presence is more valuable than the propositions intended to lead us there is obvious. It is far more valuable to arrive at a destination than to make a career of reading road signs.

Paul must have been remembering the bloody campaign he had waged against the followers of The Way when he writes that "the letter kills, but the Spirit gives life." (2 Corinthians 3.6). I would state this truth in somewhat less violent language. Perhaps this would go down easier: "As corn kernels are more nourishing than the cob, so is the Spirit to the letter." But I am not writing to a network of new churches filled with pagans and lapsed Jews scattered all over Asia Minor who needed forceful language to 'get it.'

In evangelism the point of the spear is charismatic ministry

Imagine it is about 30 A.D. and you are a disciple of Yeshua Bar Joseph. This makes you one of the twelve most privileged men to ever breathe in the long history of mankind. You are spending weeks, whole blocks of time in the presence of a man so captivating that every day raises a question you have never before pondered. Everything you have believed from childhood is malleable to this man. Nothing remains sacred unless he touches it. Nothing of the religion which has surrounded you from birth remains holy unless he first reshapes it and returns it to you throbbing with a life force you dare not refuse.

Today begins like so many others. Last night you slept in an orchard, falling asleep in a tumble of your friends while still hungry of spirit. But now, hungry of body, you thirteen enter the next village to hunt breakfast and to look for where the daily traffic will be heavy. Having found the hub of human activity you notice the same pattern you have seen before. The mothers, especially those followed by maiden girls, give you a wide berth. The men are cautious but polite.

Within minutes, however, children are everywhere, grabbing your robe, the little ones begging to be picked up, laughing, chattering, drawn to Yeshua like iron filings to a magnet. Rabbi finds a place to sit. In moments he is the calm center of a gaggle of children. There is one under each arm, a third on his lap. He talks little because the love and tenderness that shine from him is a language all its own, his touch a dialect the children know by instinct. You know to not hinder them; the pointed rebuke you once received after shooing some away was a sharp lesson learned.

On the edge of the bouncing circle of children is a nine

year-old leaning on his single crutch, the wooden helper for his crooked leg, his handicap as real as a fence beyond which he can only watch normal childhood. Rabbi sees him and his gaze brings tears to the child's eyes. They're not the bitter tears that have stung him so often when he was ignored, rebuked, teased, or dismissed. These are sweet tears overflowing from a shrunken heart now filling with love.

Rabbi calls to him and the other children part to make a path for him to stump his way to the one who holds him with his eyes. A hush stills everyone; today all the snickering, all the cat calls are silenced. Rabbi strokes his hair gently, then touches his leg. The crutch falls with a clatter to the ground and the child, at a nod, turns and runs pell mell for mother and home. For the first time in his life he jumps over a basket in the door path and shouting with a joy he can not contain bursts through the door.

And it's still early morning. All day they come, some led because they're blind, some carried on a cot, some limping, some shuffling. Every one, *every one*, leaves happy. But Rabbi says little. He allows the cries of rejoicing to rise and fall and he never so much as raises a hand to silence the wonder. And over one or two or three days the ground is made ready. It is broken up as the children are restored first. The soil is then conditioned as the old ones are released from the bondage of pain. Then the ground is planted by the gentleness of Rabbi's responses to initial hostility, fertilized with questions of his own, and watered by the commendable behavior of his disciples. *And when demonstrated power over nature and heaven's glory shining in his eyes have given him an audience, he then begins to teach, to harvest, to gather.*

Rabbi Yeshua gave us an ideal to follow. It was an irrepressible force 2,000 years ago, producing such a wave of favor it would have drowned him had not angels fortified him again and again. And it proves as effective today wherever it is tried.

EPILOGUE

In the spring of 2013 the frequency and graphic intensity I had experienced during five years of encounters with Mariah moved quietly into the background. There has been a tranquil pause before Sheryl and I return to the familiar role of students, this time at the Bethel School of Supernatural Ministry in Redding, CA.

It has not been felt as a loss nor is there any sense of abandonment, but a question did rise up. My spirit asked the eternally dumb question, "Lord, why? Are you done talking to me directly? Will there be no further dramatic encounters?"

Ever faithful, His response was immediate.

"Do you want to get married again?"

"No! The significance of that one-time event could never be duplicated. To pledge myself twice and so publicly to the same woman would mock the nearly 50 years of covenant between us!"

"Well . . . ?"

As blunt as it may sound, I am convinced that life without the presence of that lively Spirit who has provoked what is recalled above could never be more than marriage would be without sex. Partnership without intimacy is an unfulfilled life. I have come to appreciate why marriage and analogies to sexual experience (as in the Old Testament *Song of Solomon*) are used so often in scripture to suggest the passion that seizes us in fellowship with the Father and with Holy Spirit. Like a captivating woman, God can not be owned and any conclusions about His purposes and methods will expand as soon as you adopt them.

I repeat: our first duty to God is to allow Him to love us. And however intimate our relationship with Him may be, there will always be a veil that seduces us into pursuing more. God is urgent in His desire to be recognized and just as urgent that we shall never be able to boast that we know Him fully. Therefore, be satisfied with the love He offers for love is its own excuse.

Usefulness, with which ambition seeks to clothe itself, is a consequence, not an objective. If obedience or scholarship or virtue is to have any value it must follow and never precede the receiving of Grace. When this sequence is respected the human will can never metastasize and deform the human spirit.

RECEIVED IN WORSHIP

Along with experience in a new dimension there has been an introduction to a much more active worship style. While more spontaneous and wider in expression than the style I was familiar with, worship with charismatics is, nevertheless, a developed art form. Worship is so important it is given priority of place. It is never less than celebration and the time it occupies often seems inadequate. At times it breaks free and the singing and praise may go on for another hour or more. They joke at Bethel Church that when revival began about 20 years ago they brought watches to the Sunday night service only to watch the calendar roll over to Monday.

I have come to expect certain things. The open area in front of the stage is packed as densely as a disco dance floor, the worshipers, hands raised, eyes closed, letting themselves sway in rhythm with the band. If there is someone prostrate in the aisle or praying, forehead to the carpet, all is perfectly normal. The volume is high enough that any notes sung out of tune are buried so deeply in the communal sound no one else will hear it. I may not even hear my own voice. Joy alone reigns and I'll happily duck the swinging arms of the young woman in the row ahead of me who's twirling and dancing in place. "I'm chasing you, Yahweh!" Who would stop her?

Something quite peculiar often seizes me in this holy place where worship thrives. About 20 minutes in, there is such a backlog of thought and emotion I feel a nearly physical pressure. Words demand out and standing is delay. A dam cracks as old restraints of formality weaken. The notebook is opened; I consent to sit while 1500 people remain standing. I prick the dam with my pen point and let tumble the words. It is my necessary act of worship.

HEART SPEAK

I sang full voice
Adding to the thunder of worship saints have found.

I whispered on my bed
While Spirit floated past,
And with her sleep was sound.

I wrote my heart to a distant friend
And words I could not say were still a flush of light.

My greeting shone on a hope-starved stranger
And out of only kindness
He glimpsed the edges of his night.

Faint or full,
With or without word
My heart cries out to Father,
For me and Spirit, laughing,
Dance a waltz to the world absurd.

WE WORSHIP

We worship

Wrapped in draperies of rhythm,
    pulsing tapestries of sound,

While, brush by brush, the dream weavers color
    image from the music,

And the dancers twist and leap
    saluting we who need a mirror
      for our rising hearts.

We worship

To still the anguish of the suffering we saw
    beside us in the silent market aisle;

To cleanse the soul of the surfeit of desire to spend
    what we have not for what we need not.

We worship

Because, we children once weak grown bold,
    pray until we ask, then ask until we cry,
      then cry until

We worship.

WORSHIP TILL IT'S WILD!

This is that which makes men wonder,
  A cry from every aching heart

For a speaking role in heaven's play,
  Since all may have a part.

To full from empty,
  From never to now.

To color from black;
  And from can't to knowing how.

Life within life until
  The shadows bow to light.

Spirit lifting high as heaven
  Giving victory before the fight.

No praise is too extreme,
  No prophet failing to surprise;

No move to bless or to obey
  That does not reach His eyes.

Worship till it's wild!

THE MEASURE OF WORSHIP

Long, the desire that carries me here,
  Deep, the need I know;
High, the hope that follows witness,
  Wide, the welcome to which I go.

Beyond myself I hear the whisper,
  "Come in; the rest of you is here.
Behind, are all the hurts disarmed,
  Ahead, your native royalty appears."

Move, see safe and challenge merge;
  Stand still, but all your cell songs ring.
Silence is but a waiting stage for wonder;
  In measures vast does worship sing.

FRIDAY NIGHT HIGH

An unbroken line from Churn Creek
    Up the hill they come;
From eighteen to eighty years, sensing soul food,
    Moving to the net
That sweeps the hungry to the feast.

Music throbs the corporate heart beat –
    Anchor and agent
        Grounding and lifting
            Fertile and fruit.

The leader throws out the challenge –
    "Overstate God's goodness if you can!"
A prophets' congress declares the brooding blessing
    From sight outside their own, in words
    they alone can hear.

So it forms, at once anew and old,
    Mariah's playful syndicate,
Subversive to darkness, a window to light.
    Each heart a fashioned instrument of praise
Finding its place, an orchestra of joys.
    Worship born in concert and Glory held.

CREATION'S SONG

If the earth would carry rhythm,
    If the sky could cry;
If every waterway sang along its course
    It would be the sound of worship, full and high.

But where are those, formed last, made first to lead;
    The conductors, mumbling,
      searching for their place?
Flailing with dissonance, not sure of rhyme or key,
    The song unsung until, eyes up,
      they see God's face?

When Adam's children hear as heard,
    When Earth's groans are stilled at willing cost;
The anthem then will finally be joined,
    Worship whole, again in tune, not one note lost.

APPENDIX A

EVERSON

The following is the most unusual and extensive of all the encounters I have had to date. I have included it only because it is possible that some of the scenes are in fact symbolic of events yet to occur or are graphic parables of forces now at play in the world. I make no claim to authoritative prophetic insight and was myself in awe of the dramatic content. I did not expect what was received and have no reason to expect more.

THE FOUR COMPASS POINTS
FEBRUARY 17, 2012

The evening of the 16th Sheryl and I had been invited to the home of Glen and Barbara Hjort to enjoy a pizza supper and meet Roy Kendall. Roy is an accomplished musician and a powerful charismatic pastor who has been living in Israel for 21 years. His ministry is primarily the teaching of worship practices to those groups in Israel who acknowledge Jesus as Lord or Messiah and whose numbers have grown from less than 50 groups in 1990 to over 350 today.

As he finished leading us in worship with his inspired piano playing and his marvelous voice I was given a brief vision of the face of a very large compass with only the four principal points in bold black letters. With this came an urgency to declare in a strong voice the will of God over the earth with the following declarations:

Say to the north, Victory!
Say to the east, Peace!
Say to the south, Sweetness!
Say to the west, Glory!

As we together made these decrees there was a felt presence in the room, an agreement of the Spirit that we were speaking the heart of the Father.

It is now early in the morning of the 17th. The first of several scenes that I saw in an active vision (a spirit encounter in which I can ask questions) was of a similar small group worshiping. I did not recognize who was

APPENDIX A

there. I was on my knees praying with my forehead on the floor. The group had just with great energy spoken the decrees of the four points of the compass. The Spirit of the Lord filled the room, rising in a crescendo and peaking as together we cried "Glory!" to the west. Everyone fell out under the power of God. Sheryl fell to her left on to the couch where I had been sitting and as she lay under the anointing she began to speak in a prayer language. When the Spirit lifted Sheryl continued to speak in her new prayer language as if it had always been part of her.

Immediately the scene shifted to a large auditorium filled with hundreds of people. It seemed that it was the same convention center where the Spiritual Hunger conference is held every September in Spokane. I had been the speaker. As I came to the end of whatever I had presented I led the group to declare the points of the compass. As the group shouted "Glory!" to the west the room became charged with the presence of the Spirit and a great number fell out under the anointing. Some were weeping, some were laughing, rocking side to side on the floor, some were singing or dancing while others moaned, groaned, or shouted praises. It was holy pandemonium.

An attendee in a wheelchair near the platform to my right came out of his seat as if the chair were spring-loaded and began to run around the room. Suddenly, there was a rumble of thunder in the room and a blast of light. It began to rain gently on everyone though no rain fell on the carpets or the chairs and while everyone got wet, no one was soaked. Spontaneous singing in the Spirit broke out and went on until the scene faded. My eyes were opened and I saw hundreds of angels in the room. Everyone on the floor under the anointing had an angel standing over him or kneeling beside him. They were ministering angels assigned to individually transmit a blessing to anyone prostrate under the power of God.

And that scene ended.

I was then taken to a board room where a group of ten or so were seated around a conference table. It was a Thursday afternoon and the group was listening to me summarize what to expect that weekend in the university church where I had been invited to speak. I was a graduate of the theological seminary housed on the campus and mutual friends had secured the invitation. I explained to them that the morning worship service was a setup for the evening meeting which would begin at 7:00. They would see no ecstatic manifestations in the morning nor any personal ministry at the end of the service. But they should be prepared to leave the building open for the evening service until at least 1:00 or 2:00 in the morning and perhaps until daybreak the next day.

There was now a brief scene from the close of the morning service. I had no sense of what I had said but the Spirit lay over the congregation like a blanket and you could hear a pin drop. Some appeared to be having a hard time breathing while some others had a hardened, fixed expression of anger on their faces and when I sat down these last began to leave the church before the final hymn was sung.

Then I was taken to the final moments of the evening service. The sanctuary was standing room only. I was coming to the climax of my sermon during which, while not a direct rebuke, I had without reservation called on the organization to give to the Holy Spirit the place it must have. If they did not, their church would see God's final work bypass them to be carried out by those who could not boast of the privileges and heritage they rightfully honor.

As I led the audience to declare the four points of the compass the Spirit drove through the atmosphere like a wind storm as over 2,000 voices shouted "Glory!" to the west. What now occurred was nearly a repeat of the former large group scene, but this time the variety of manifestations were taking place among a group of people who had no grid for this whatsoever. Consequently, there was an innocence, a purity to their response that must have delighted the Spirit for there was a sense in the atmosphere of swirling, dancing angels laughing at what they had provoked.

While I stood observing from the platform I heard the sound of approaching emergency vehicles. The side entrance at the front of the church to my left opened and several firemen in their fighting suits and several policemen burst into the room looking for the fire reported to them. I asked if they were referring to the pillar of fire above the roof outside. Astonished, they asked me how I knew what was seen from outside if I was inside. I simply smiled. One of the firemen collapsed against the door frame and one of the policemen crumpled to the floor. A buddy for each of these fallen men found a place on the first pew to wait for their friends to come around and the rest quietly returned to their stations.

Well, there was no way I could be heard above the volume of worshiping voices so I began to circulate among the congregation. Stepping over bodies I slowly made my way up the aisle. As I would lay my hand on some to pray for them they would go down, as helpless as rag dolls. Filled with the joy of the Lord I listened to the murmur of hundreds praying softly in the Spirit, almost all of them in a prayer language they had received only moments before. Under this layer of sound was another layer, a sound of water tumbling over rocks mixed with the sighing of a breeze in the trees. It was the sound of a word, the word 'Shalom.'

And over these two layers of sound was a third; the organ was being played with a skill and a genius beyond any human talent. Intrigued, I turned around to see the organ apparently playing by itself as the organist was flat out on the floor behind his bench. As I continued to puzzle over what I was seeing my eyes were opened. I saw an angel at the console so full of the glory of the music he seemed from behind to be in a trance. But then he turned around to catch my gaze and there was a radiant smile on his face. I refer to the angel as 'he' because that is the default of our language but I couldn't determine a gender. This was the most beautiful creature I had ever seen. The beauty was not from the surface, it was deep and it made you want to weep and shout at the same time for having seen such a beautiful thing even once.

And then the scene ended.

Next I was taken to Washington, D.C. where I found myself on the mall looking toward the capital in the distance. An earthquake was shaking the capital, not a physical shaking but a spasm in a spiritual dimension. Without knowing the place or when it had occurred, I was made to understand that there had been a nuclear device detonated somewhere among the nations and enormous damage had been inflicted. All the governments of earth were trembling, not knowing what the balance of powers would become and who would now be allied with whom. The Lord was taking the opportunity to cleanse our government with His fury.

I felt His jealousy for the country over which His Spirit had been so powerful in its formation. This nation is His peculiar treasure, His personal possession, and He will no longer tolerate corruption in high places. The recklessness of a powerful elite who will not act from principle but only for political advantage is confronted by His purity. The tolerance of abortion that murders the most innocent among us in the service of sexual license is parallel to the worship of heathen idols in ancient times. Though it is the law of the land it is a fearful affront to God and He will no longer tolerate those who excuse it. I see dozens of the powerful fleeing the city to escape the wrath of God. I see only one face, that of a prominent politician, the face a mask of anger mixed with disdain.

I am then taken to New York City. I am standing on Wall Street looking up at what appear to be canyon walls; the skyscrapers in which are the great investment houses that fix and trade the wealth of the nations. On the windows in my view I see the reflections of the windows of the facing buildings, a perfect symbol of the uniformity of practice on the street. As I watch, a wind sweeps up the street with the force of a winter storm carrying the dread of plague within it. The spirit of the street freezes as all of these money changers realize in a moment the enormity of their sin in handling God's money while never acknowledging His rule.

The computer monitors go berserk as control over capital is lost. Vast sums of money disappear with neither a paper trail nor an electronic signature. Staggering amounts of money appear in the bank accounts of the most humble, anonymous children of God. Great rejoicing spreads among God's true church as these ones, unknown to the world, indulge in a celebration of giving such as the world has never seen. I see financial provision run like fresh streams of water into desert regions, filling every low place, finding new water courses to run in and then overflowing the banks, spreading life-giving water over a large area. The native populations run out of their crude houses and splash in the water, laughing with joy.

What follows is a most remarkable sight. I see the country of North Korea as on a large wall map. As I watch, the earth opens and swallows the country's entire leadership and much of the military. It is made clear to me that the country has been ruled so completely by demonic forces acting through dictators that there is no hope of redemption.

The first reaction by the tens of millions now without a government is a paroxysm of weeping as the cumulative anxieties, the fear piled on fear, thrust on them by those who controlled every detail of their lives are shed in a moment. The light of God's true purpose for them chases away the decades of conditioning to which they have been subjected. What follows is a celebration of freedom that leaves the nation giddy with joy.

I next see the country of Japan. Compared with what is happening throughout the rest of the world Japan is protected by a spirit of peace. They have been a hard people to evangelize with Christianity but God has been at work within their Buddhism and ancestor worship to shape them into a nation bound to each other with cords of compassion and a deep understanding of mercy. Their open hearts, so willing to comfort and aid each other, is the divinely-fashioned legacy of their suffering from nuclear warfare. This peace is the reward for their perseverance.

One place in Japan does not please God: the Ginza district of Tokyo. This showplace for materialism has been a cancer on their soul. God's focus is on the garish lighting for which it is famous, the neon clamor for the affections of men when what is offered are mere toys. As a rebuke, all the lights in the district go out at once. God pulls the plug and the spirit of materialism that was celebrated there evaporates in an instant.

And so the vision finally ended.

APPENDIX B

RAVI: BEYOND "NO"

As mentioned above, one of the striking features of historical encounters with God has been the reflex to argue with God, to refuse a directive, and to generally forget who's in charge. This was true not only for Balaam, who was in open rebellion against his heaven-sent orders, but is also true for those who are wonderfully used and who, in general, cooperate with the work of the Holy Spirit. God is not always a gentleman and He may at any time draw us beyond the normal limits of our faith to do what is fraught with a hazard we can't believe He's asking us to accept.

In the following story there is a remarkable resemblance to an encounter related in the book of Acts, chapter 8, beginning with verse 26. It's the experience of Philip presenting the gospel as seen through the prism of Isaiah to the treasurer of the queen of Ethiopia. Note these similarities:

- There is a supernatural, voice-activated encounter between the evangelist and a stranger.
- There is a short, simple presentation of the essence of the gospel.
- The message is immediately accepted and the new believer is baptized into fellowship with the church.
- The evangelist and his convert are abruptly separated and the new believer moves forward in faith with no further instruction. With only the assistance of the Holy Spirit, the expression of faith in the new people group to which the gospel is carried will be culturally appropriate. I believe this sets a standard for efficient and effective evangelism, a method for advancing the Kingdom of God under the best circumstances for growth.

The following experience is told by Darren Wilson in his book *Filming God.* In the book he tells the fascinating back story of producing his trilogy of dramatic documentaries (*The Finger of God, Furious Love, and Father of Lights*) that highlight the often startling initiatives of God's Spirit in our day. In *Father of Lights*, Darren features the itinerant ministry of Ravi, a former Indian drug dealer and gang leader now become an evangelist. The following account is excerpted from pages 179-189.

I've never met anyone remotely like Ravi. Sure, I've met scores of people who claim they speak to God on a regular basis, that He tells them what to do, that He has even visited them on occasion, but Ravi is wholly unique due to the fact that he hears the audible voice of God speaking directly to him every day.

So quite often Ravi will find himself having to do something that is entirely out of his comfort zone, or very strange, and he will never see the reason he was told to do such a thing. It is a tough life, but one that is built on the trust that God loves him as His son, and he is not simply a hired hand to do His bidding.

He told me a story he lovingly refers to as "the train story." This will give you an idea of what it might be like for you if God decided to bestow this unique gift of hearing His audible voice on a regular basis. Be careful what you wish for . . .

Ravi was traveling to a conference in India put on by some American evangelists. He was going to hear the teaching, yes, but he was mostly going for the food. At this point in his life, Ravi had very little money, and the prospect of getting some good eats while hearing the Word of God preached was simply too much to pass up. So he donned his best white shirt, complete with intricate embroidery across the breast (to hear him tell it, this was the greatest shirt ever made. In reality, it was the only nice shirt he owned!), hopped on a train, and cracked open his Bible to read during the journey.

About halfway through the train ride, he heard that familiar voice of Daddy.

"Jump off the train."

His first instinct was to rebuke that evil spirit in Jesus' name. And that's just what he did. But the voice kept speaking, and it was a voice he knew well.

"Jump off the train. I want you to jump off the train." Ravi began to have an argument with God. The train was going fast, and as he looked out the window, he resolved that there was no way he was going to do what Daddy was asking this time. This wasn't a request, it was suicide.

Yet the voice persisted. "Jump. Jump. Jump . . ."

He tried to ask God why He wanted him to jump off the train.

"Just jump."

He tried to show God what He obviously wasn't realizing. Ravi may not die in the jump, but he would certainly be grievously injured. How could God be glorified if that happened?

"Just jump."

"Ask somebody else to jump."

For 20 minutes Ravi argued with God. He tried to bargain with God. Not once did the Lord ever tell him why He was asking Ravi to do this. He just expected obedience based on trust from His friend.

Reluctantly, Ravi got up from his seat, Bible in tow, and went out of the train car onto the landing linking the two cars together. The Indian countryside whizzed by him, and the roar of the wheels on the track was deafening. Was the train speeding up? God, I'm going to die if I do this.

"Just jump."

He wasn't going to do it. He couldn't do it. He was frozen to the spot. What is the point of doing this, he kept asking himself. He still wondered if it was the devil trying to trick him, but it couldn't be; he knew that voice too well. He had heard it since he became a Christian at age 17.

Suddenly, as if Jesus Himself were standing directly behind him, the voice screamed in his ear, "Jump now!" and he felt two hands push him, hard, off the train.

I never asked Ravi what he was thinking as he flew through the air at that moment. My guess is, before he hit the ground, the lone thought was something along the lines of, Who the heck just pushed me?! That thought would have been swallowed up immediately by the impact his body made when it hit the . . . mud?

Ravi didn't realize it when he was standing on the train, but at the exact moment he jumped, the train was passing a construction site. There had been a lot of rain lately, and along the edge of this construction area a giant pool of mud and water had collected near the bottom of the train tracks. Ravi jumped (or was pushed, depending on how you look at it) at the exact moment this pool of mud came into view. He landed in the soft mud and, as he puts it, was "baptized in mud." This wasn't a high church sprinkling on the head, this was full-on, Bible-belt submersion. He came up gasping for air and watched as the last car of the train snarled away from him. He then looked down and remembered what shirt he was wearing. There was no washing machine in the world that would get out this stain.

"Great. Thanks a lot, God, look what you did to my shirt!" I believe that was his first reaction. It wasn't until he was slowly pulling himself out of the mud pit that he noticed . . . the other guy, 30 feet away, who was doing the same thing.

They regarded each other carefully, until Ravi was the first to voice what they were obviously both thinking.

"Hey, did you just jump off that train?"

"Yes," the man replied.

"Why did you do that?"

"I was trying to kill myself," was his simple reply. "Why

did you jump?"

"Don't ask," was all Ravi said. It was bad enough that God had ruined his shirt, he wasn't about to make himself look like a complete idiot.

As they both exited the mud pit, Ravi knew why the Lord had pushed him off the train at that precise moment. It was for this guy. God knew this guy was in such a bad place that he was going to try to kill himself, and since Ravi was on the train, He would be God's instrument of hope for this man.

The only problem was, Ravi wasn't entirely excited with God at the moment. He definitely wasn't going to get to the conference in time to get some good food, and his best shirt had just been completely destroyed. Plus, come on, the Lord had just pushed him off a moving train!

Realizing that he would either do this thing or the whole ordeal would be for nothing, he approached the man and began telling him about Jesus. Of course, as Ravi puts it, he preached to the man "very angrily." This wasn't what he wanted to be doing at the moment, but he did it because he knew he was supposed to. So he presented the Gospel of love while malice overtook his heart, but the man heard every word and eagerly asked to accept Jesus as his Savior.

This didn't really affect Ravi the way the Lord maybe hoped it would, because he was still furious. His job now officially done, he then saw a nearby pond where they both might be able to rinse some of this mud off. As they walked over to it, Ravi grudgingly asked the man another question.

"Hey, do you want to be baptized?"

"What is 'baptized'?" was the man's reply.

"Don't worry about it, just come with me."

Ravi baptized him, thus washing the man's sins away along with the mud. They shook hands and parted ways, Ravi called some friends who lived nearby and they picked him up, gave him clothes to borrow, and he arrived at the conference three hours late.

The other man had walked off to begin his new life.

Months later, Ravi was attending yet another conference.

He felt a tap on his shoulder and turned to see a man smiling at him.

"Can I help you?" he asked.

"Pastor, do you not remember me? I was the one who jumped off the train with you awhile back."

"Oh yes, yes," Ravi replied, "how could I forget!"

"I wanted to thank you for introducing me to Jesus, and I wanted you to know that I went back to my village that very day and began preaching about Him to my friends and family. Today I am the pastor of my village, and it is all because you jumped off that train with me at the same time! Is God amazing or what?"

Ravi hugged the man and wished him well. He then went to a quiet place and cried his eyes out. He repented for not trusting his Father, for yelling at Him, for preaching His message of love out of anger. And he promised the Lord that if He ever asks him to jump off a train again, he will do it with gusto.